Content

Ross Dungan

methuen | drama
LONDON • NEW YORK • OXFORD • NEW DELHI • SYDNEY

METHUEN DRAMA
Bloomsbury Publishing Plc
50 Bedford Square, London, WC1B 3DP, UK
1385 Broadway, New York, NY 10018, USA
29 Earlsfort Terrace, Dublin 2, Ireland

BLOOMSBURY, METHUEN DRAMA and the Methuen
Drama logo are trademarks of Bloomsbury Publishing Plc

First published in Great Britain 2024

A catalogue record for this book is available from the British Library.

A catalog record for this book is available from the Library of Congress.

ISBN: PB: 978-1-3505-4321-8
ePDF: 978-1-3505-4322-5
eBook: 978-1-3505-4323-2

Series: Modern Plays

Typeset by Mark Heslington Ltd, Scarborough, North Yorkshire

To find out more about our authors and books visit
www.bloomsbury.com and sign up for our newsletters.

Content

by Ross Dungan

Alan Joshua McEneaney
Alannah Genevieve Hulme Beaman
Tina Janet Moran
Craig/Dr Collins/Trevor Aidan Moriarty
Jean/Georgina/Lauren Roisin O'Mahony
Voiceover Kate Kennedy and Bryan Moriarty

Director: Sara Joyce
Set & Lighting Design: Ciaran Bagnall
Costume Design: Catherine Fay
Sound Design & Composition: Sinead Diskin
Video Designer: Eoin Robinson
Illustrations & Graphic Design: Sarah Moloney
Movement Director: Philip Connaughton
Production Manager: Eoin Kilkenny
Stage Manager: Evie McGuinness
Assistant Stage Manager: Sarah Purcell
Assistant Production Manager: Laura Murphy
Chief Electrician: Suzie Cummins
Chief Audio-visual: Laura Rainsford
Deputy Sound Design: Martha Knight
Costume Supervisor: Suzanne Sheehan
Crew: Damien Woods, John Norton
Co-Producers: Sarah Byrne, Matthew Smyth + Ois O'Donoghue
Production Photography: Ste Murray

Developed with the assistance of The Arts Council

Content

Characters

Laurence	Dr Collins
Alan	Tristan
Jean	Dry Cleaner
Alannah	Ollie
Craig	Repair Person
Georgina	Trevor
Tina	Lauren

Author's Note

Illustration – *The idea is that all the drawing should be live and done in real time. The specificity of the style and what they should depict are purposefully vague in the stage directions. This is largely down to my certainty that an illustrator will invariably come up with better ideas than I ever could.*

Jean – *It's not always specified when Jean enters and exits scenes. There can and should be some freedom and play with Jean's presence on stage.*

Content – *No traumatic content should ever be displayed on stage or shown to an audience. The content should always be abstracted in some capacity.*

Voiceover – *The original production used voiceover and a `Voice of the Internet' to support moments when text from the internet is being displayed.*

SimOne.Says Posts – *Each post from SimOne.Says where a 'contestant' is named should have a flag emoji of the country of the contestant (e.g. 'Tonight's Contestant is 24 Forest G' should have an Irish flag after the name).*

Podcast – *Beginning on page 40, the story from a 'podcast or something' that Alannah tells is taken from a real-life segment from Episode 205 of* This American Life. *The story is written and reported by the brilliant Jonathan Goldstein.*

A note on the original cast and creatives – *Finally, it cannot be overstated the cumulative effect that the cast and creatives have had on shaping this work. As is ever the way, the best bits are theirs.*

For Matt,
Our Moon

Act One

Laurence *arrives home. He sets up a stand. Places his phone on it. He brings in a couple of holdall bags containing various bits of equipment. Headphones on, he takes his phone off the stand. Rewatches something on it. Types something in. Hits send.*

He goes back to the camera set-up. A deep breath. Lights out.

Scene One

Alan *is alone on stage. A moment of anxiety. It builds. And then . . .*

. . . He steps into a tranquil space. After a moment, a person in a full-size kangaroo suit enters. This is **Jean**. **Jean** *reaches into their pouch. Pulls out a notebook. Hands it to* **Alan**.

Alan Thanks.

With **Jean** *helming it, a drawing starts behind* **Alan**. *It contains no black or white.*

Alan It happened a few months back. Before the August bank holiday. We work the bank holiday obviously. I don't think I told you about any of this at the time.

A gesture from **Jean**: *'I'm all ears/You can tell me now.'*

The drawing continues, populating the world of an office.

Alan That morning, in the break room, some of the guys – they were talking about her before she came in. Alannah. I've maybe mentioned her before? My former colleague? (*Off* **Jean**'s *nod.*) Right. (*He gets back to it.*) She had this thing where she'd always seem to know if she'd just been talked about. She'd walk in and be all like, 'Please, please don't stop on my account.' And then when no one said anything, she'd call them something under her – well, *over* her breath. Like, one day she called them a – do you mind if I swear? (*A* **Jean** *head shake.*) –'a bunch of rubber-dicked, rubberneckers'. (*Looks to* **Jean**.) She used to do this job. A . . . 'girls in your area' type thing. They liked . . . discussing it. And that morning when Alannah came in, the guys they see her and shut up. But this time she said nothing. Locked her phone in her locker and went on out. I mean, maybe she just had her earbuds in. But I've thought about that. Since.

Alan *continues to draw. A series of cubicles and workstations.*

Out on the floor, I always select the workstation that's as far away from the vending machine as possible.

Alan's *cubicle is circled.*

Cos that's where people congregate and there can be a bit of noise. Which is fine. It is. I just think it's important to create the best environment for concentration. And that . . . that's where Alannah was.

Another cubicle is circled, across from **Alan**'s. *Beat.*

It was about four hours into our shift when I heard her. Sometimes you do overhear people. It's hard for them *not* to respond at times to what they see. Could be a big breath. Might get an 'f-ing hell' or . . . yeah, sometimes if people, if they can't hold it in until they get to the stairwell, they might have a bit of a cry right there. At their workstation. But all things considered, it's fairly quiet most of the time. So, when Alannah does this kind of . . . *bark*. It's a bit unusual. And then . . . she runs from the monitor. To the break room. And she – because she's a bit frantic – she can't get the combo right for her locker. And the vending machine crowd – most of the floor actually – they sort of slowly drift towards the break-room door. To watch. And I don't know *exactly* how long it took her to get the phone and make the call. (*Seeing* **Jean**'s *confusion.*) Oh, I don't know cos I wasn't there by then. I'd gone straight to her workstation. To see what she'd seen.

Beat. The drawing moves to a screen monitor.

And I don't want this to sound how it sounds, what was on her screen would be immensely hard viewing for anyone. But for footage showing a person ceasing their life via suicide it wasn't *particularly* graphic. A blond-haired guy, early thirties. Hoodie. Non-violent. And a lot of that stuff would be funnelled my way, it's sort of – as you know – my area of expertise in there. Content arising from suicide and pro-mortalism forums. Alannah mostly works the spam queue but it still can't have been the first time she's seen something like this. So, I'm trying to figure out why *this* one – a blond guy in his sitting room – why it's so . . . tricky. I get to the break room and she's – yeah – by now she's smashed up her locker door and thrown her phone across the room. And – . . . (*Re-evaluating.*) Now, I can't remember if this happened *exactly* this way because it does seem a bit too . . . *cinematic.* But I remember seeing her phone. Which had splintered quite badly. And she was still calling him. So his face came up on the screen. Blond. Early thirties. The same guy from the video. Her brother. Her twin actually, as I later found out. Laurence.

Beat.

She'd thought what she watching was live. Because it was a – well – it was a livestream. But it was a repost of it. Was maybe about five hours old at that point. It was still bright outside in the video. I don't know what specific thing made her realise he was already gone but by the time of the phone throwing . . . she had.

Beat.

She went pretty quiet then. Just . . . sat. And in the quiet, some people around me, they sort of lapse in conversation. About how there's 500 million new social media posts worldwide every day. Likelihood of her getting that ticket . . . a one in 500 million chance, they say. Then someone says cos we're straddling night and day shifts, they say it's technically closer to one in a *billion*. And I want to do something helpful. But what I say is that she should have a glass of water. Not even pouring some and bringing it over, just suggesting – you know – to stay hydrated. Generally. And . . . eventually, she gets up, gets her bag, hasn't ever come back. I've felt bad about that. Awful. Since it happened. And, and, and –

He works himself up. **Jean** *moves closer to* **Alan**. *Doing deep breathing together, he successfully calms. And then . . .*

Alan   Thanks.

Beat.

She was kinda in my dream this afternoon.

Jean *indicates to* **Alan***: 'Please go on/I'd like to hear more.'*

Alan   Well . . . we're still at work. But – in the dream – our office is, like, this crumbling lighthouse.

The style of the drawing changes. More flickering. A lighthouse is depicted.

And I can hear her wrecking up the place again. And . . . I realise . . . that this time I know what to say to her. And even *though* it's only a dream, I'm still . . . do you mind if I swear again? (*Shake of the head from* **Jean**.) I'm just absolutely *panicking*. Sorry. I actually forgot to swear that time. But to ensure I say it right – in the same way we triage content in work, I break it into steps.

Each step is listed on the screen as **Alan** *says it:*

Step 1: *Identify Yourself.* (*Practising, nervous.*) Hi, former colleague. Alan Kenedy. One 'n' in Kenedy. One 'n' in 'Alan', also.

Step 2: *Relay Shared Family Experience.* Eh . . . Self-explanatory.

Step 3: *Be Factual and Succinct.* Yes, your brother's video was awful. But it carried a digital footprint. A unique one. And because it's now been flagged, if someone reposts it, there's a high probability it'll be automatically deleted. AI can even catch those ones. It won't be seen again. Cos if someone is contemplating suicide, a video like your brother's one can create a . . . *momentum*. But now . . . he won't. That momentum, it stops with him.

Step 4: *Make Yourself Available Should She Have Any Follow-Up Questions*. Again, self-explanatory.

And so, I'm standing next to dream Alannah. And I know now . . . what it is that I have to say. And then . . . this other thought came. That maybe she doesn't want to be bothered. By me. Right then. Maybe I'm not the right person to . . . For it all. And so . . . I just stay quiet.

A zoom out of all his drawings from the scene.

Jean . . . do you think what I do is important?

A nod from **Jean.**

Alan   Yeah. No, I know. And it's not like I'm . . . reversing climate change here, but I'm – . . . I am part of a solution to something. I know I can help and the help is helpful. But sometimes I worry that if my blip was showing up on, like, a radar. With all the other blips. That people wouldn't really notice, you know, if it sort of . . . slid off the screen. I guess part of me has been wondering . . . am I making a difference? Am I adding . . . value?

He can barely say the word 'value'. Beat.

Actually – . . . You know what. I think I just needed to ask that. Cos I'm – actually – no, I'm feeling better about it. Already.

Jean *points to a drawing of* **Alannah.**

Alan   . . . Sorry? (*Getting it.*) Oh, Alannah? Well she's . . . long gone. So saying any of that now. It's moot, I think. Yeah. (*Checks the time.*) Eh . . . It's almost midnight, I should probably . . . get a move on. Probably all a bit . . . juvenile isn't it? This. (*A shake of the head from* **Jean**.) Yeah, no. A good bit more . . . centred now. Thanks. As always.

Alan *walks forward and . . .*

Scene Two: Work

. . . Suddenly, we're at **Alan***'s work. On the content-moderation work floor known as the 'abattoir'. As he logs onto his workstation, it displays the company slogan: 'Thank You for Making the Internet Safer'. And then . . .*

A projection of a flagged post. Onto **Alan***. It's pixelated. Colourful. These are the mostly inoffensive ones. With aplomb and alacrity, he dismisses these. But then . . .*

A different type. It's pixelated. But in a stark black and white. Going by **Alan***'s micro-reaction, we realise it's an image of 'inappropriate content'. Quickly and efficiently, he deletes it. As he goes about his work,* **Craig** *arrives over.*

Craig   There he is now. Alan. AA. The Dean of Deletion. Our self-harm charm. (*Sits on corner of desk.*) Sorry, am I interrupting or – . . .? Bloody hell, my noggin mate. The ruddy day – (*Correcting.*) Well, *night*, I'm having with these fresh-off-the-bussers. Did I tell you there was a new batch starting tonight?

Alan   Yeah. I – you asked me to set up the ten workstations for them earlier.

Craig   Oh, duh. Ta again for that. But, *Jesus* . . . Right, so my office, so it shares a wall with the room where they have their instructional, right.

Alan   Oh, yeah. I think you might have told me –

Craig (*throwaway, pressing on*)   Maybe, yeah, so I hear HR Estelle start into her whole ra-ra speech. 'You lot are the last line of defence between us and the three Bs: bullying, beheadings and bestiality.' But, thing is, they force feed them

all that, send them on out for their 'trial period'. And then –
excuse my French – they can't tell a minge from a mango.

Alan (*unsure, nodding dog*)   Yeah, no. It's a lot at first, for
sure –

Craig   Guess how many points I've had to take off them?
Already tonight. Come on guess. (*As he considers.*) Are you –
sorry – are we maybe letting traffic build up a bit there, mate?

Alan   My bad.

He refocuses on his screen. **Craig** *responds approvingly to his quick
work.*

Craig   He computes, he scores. (*Back to it.*) Thirty points
taken off them. Three. Zero. But, and this – yeah this is the
better game – out of how many tickets do you reckon that
was? Tickets I yanked out and assessed at random. Come on.
Just guess. *A* guess.

Alan   . . . Eh . . . thirty?

Craig   What? No. They haven't got like every *single* one of
them wrong, mate. They haven't looked at a still of, like, *Paw
Patrol* and classified it as police brutality. It was out of 150
tickets. Thirty out of 150. One in *five* wrong. That's how
many they managed to scuzz up.

Alan   Oh. Have they switched out with the day shift, the
new batch?

Craig   What? No, they're sitting over there, might even be
able to hear me. And if so that's not me being rude, mate.
Does them no favours to rug sweep it. If they say see this as a
foot in the door at –

Their company name is *bleeped out*.

Then a *gentle* foot up the arse, that's their best pal, mate.
'Kay. As a little comparison, how many points have you
racked up across – . . . How long you been here again?

Alan   About . . . sixty months or so.

Craig   . . . five years?

Alan   Right. It's just . . . the typical employment span is about . . . three months. So – . . . Yeah, I'll just say five years –

Craig   Just say five years, mate.

Alan   Yeah, no, I will.

Georgina, *a new employee, arrives over.*

Georgina   Eh . . . sorry, I'm – sorry for interrupting.

Craig   You can stop there with the sorrying. No such thing as an interruption, it's what I'm here for . . . (*As she says her name.*) *Georgina*.

Georgina   Yeah, so there's something in a language I don't know and an image of a – . . . I'm not sure if it's a – . . . body part or – . . . yeah.

Craig   Georgina, not your fault. They should have taught you – amongst other things – how we triage this. So Step One. We 'enhance'. We zoom in –

Georgina   It's too pixelated to zoom in.

Alan   Is there a lizard mosaic on the tiles beneath it.

Georgina   Eh . . . I think so.

Alan   That's a severed arm. It's been doing the rounds. There's a . . . militia thing in happening in Sudan, I think.

Georgina   Oh . . .

Alan   But it'll actually . . . need to be deleted under the protected brands subsection. There's a fake Rolex on the wrist. It's a fundraising drive, I think.

Craig   So . . . think you need a helping hand to get rid of the helping hand? (*Off her uncertainty.*) Just a gag, Georgina. There's a reason we call this floor the abattoir. Not the morgue. A gag a day . . . (*No rhyme occurs to him.*) . . . *improves* things.

Georgina   Okay. Thanks.

She goes. Silence.

Craig   I'm all for new blood. No one's for newer blood than me. But they can do all the 'resiliency screening' they want, 'reduce' it down to their three Bs, all their *bits*. Doesn't *communicate* it. To do this, you need a doggedness, you need that bit of woof about you. I mean – . . . let's say they ask *you* to rewrite the handbook. All *fifty-five* pages. Pen in hand, how would you make them give a square of shit?

Alan   Me? Well I – . . . I . . .

Craig (*checks a message, gives his attention back*)   Sorry.

Alan (*decides against saying it*)   Yeah, no, couldn't say really.

Craig   Yeah, corporate lingo bingo, isn't it? Wait, what were we talking about? Points. Your *points*. *Yes*. Riddle me this. What's more: number of years you've been here? Or points you've accrued?

Alan   . . . probably points. But yeah, not by . . . much.

Craig   Right. And – and you hopefully won't mind me saying this – you're not exactly Johnny Fucking Brain, are you? All that lot, 'tertiary educated'. Result? Thirty corrections between nine of them.

Alan   Yeah. (*Catching it late.*) . . . Is there not ten of them, no?

Craig   Ha. Classic AA. 'I set up ten workstations. But you speak of nine. Does not compute. Ah!' Only nine are doing the instructional. Our returnee, she's done it before. (*Off his look.*) Oh wait . . . you haven't heard? It's Camgirl. Camgirl's come back for another helping.

Alan   . . . Alannah?

Craig   *Yeah.* Apparently they'd to keep her at half-salary for one quarter after her brother. 'Legal reasons'. Have to say, did *not* think she'd be darkening another workstation here again. Guess the sex workers' pension ain't what it used to be, eh? (*Off* **Alan***'s weak smile.*) Just a gag, mate. It's actually *quite* important to normalise sex work. Keeping it in the shadows, that's actually what *keeps* it dangerous.

Alan   Oh, sorry.

Craig   It's alright, not having a go. Just something to watch out for.

Alan   Are you . . . diverting certain content away from her then?

Craig   Right. So she's a competent young woman, mate, so let's not –

Alan   I mean to say . . . if it's still her old profile settings might she not possibly get tickets that are reminiscent of what . . . unfolded with her brother –

Craig   Zip.

Alan   What . . .

Craig   *It.* Wanna lift your finger *off* the megaphone there. Zip *it.*

Beat. **Alannah** *passes.* **Craig** *nods to her. She gives a non-committal gesture back. The bare minimum of friendliness. She enters the break room. Smoking her vape.*

Craig   Good shout. I'll put her on the spam queue, full time. (*Leans in a little more.*) You know, we're not having this conversation, you can give me a . . . *blink.* But have you ever tried dusting off any of her old URLs?

Alan   . . . *no.*

Craig   (*misreading his genuine denial*)   Yeah. (*Blinks between each word.*) Me. Neither. Mate. *Anyway,* you're due your fifteen in a – (*Checks his watch.*) Ooooft . . . Is it – I'm so sorry

– is it a *massive* balls to sort of count that as it there? Just tell me to fuck off if not.

Alan   No, it's alright.

Craig   You kind of – you're an eat-at-your-desker anyway, aren't you? Solid, mate, thanks.

He goes. **Alan**, *unable to stop himself, finds his gaze lingering on* **Alannah**.

Scene Three: Break Room

It's early morning. Shift over, **Alan** *enters the break room. An image flashes up. A pixelated black and white one. A representative of the day's toll. He exhales . . . takes out his notebook. As he draws, pieces of the pixelated image move around. Changes the shape. The colours. It soon resembles something more comforting . . .*

Another kangaroo. It should feel like the same process from the opening scene.

As **Alan** *finishes his ad hoc, re-balancing exercise, he gets a text. Lights up on another section of the stage.* **Tina**, *in her pyjamas, sits in the spotlight.*

Tina (*speaking her messages*)   All done, love? Upper case x.

Alan *replies. We see his typed responses.*

Alan (*speaking his messages*)   Yeah. Why you up? All okay?

Tina   All good. Bin lorry woke me.

Alan   You are going BACK to sleep tho, yeah?

Tina   Yes DOCTOR Sleep. In a sec. Breastfeeding emoji. Oops. Finger slipped. Still dozy. Cool they have that though. Upper case X.

Alan *is then pulled back to his present locale by a recently arrived* **Alannah.**

Alannah   Drink?

Alan *looks around. There's no one else in the room. Just them.*

Alannah   Would you like to go for a drink, Alan? (*Off his continued non-response, she takes out her phone.*) Siri. Define 'drink'.

Craig *enters as this is said.*

Craig   Ooh. We all tying one off? Getting an early house humpday crew going? (*Not accepting any other response.*) Sublime. AA, you are on board, right? Toast the prodigal daughter's return.

Alan *tries to get his bearings.* **Craig** *gives him a wink.*

Alan   Eh . . . yeah, I'll just be a minute. Then I'll come join in . . .

Craig   Neds. Where the house is early, and the Ned is surly.

Alan   . . . *Neds.* Yep.

Craig   Sounds like a plan, mate. (*To* **Alannah**.) Advanced party?

Alannah   . . . Sure.

Craig   Sublime. (*To* **Alan**.) Last there, first round.

He exits. **Alannah** *goes with him.*

Tina (*speaking her messages*)   Can you get eggs? But check 'em before you buy them. Magnifying glass emoji. That one *was* intentional.

Alan (*speaking his messages*)   Mum. I'm gonna be back a bit later.

Tina   Everything alright?

Beat. **Alan** *tries to make it sound as casual as possible.*

Alan   Just doing a thing. Pub. With work people.

Tina   Unicorn star eyes bitmoji.

Beat.

(*Sounding 'chill'.*) Bitmoji deletion. Sure. No biggie. *Lower* case x.

Alan *tries to compose himself.* **Jean** *arrives out. With* **Jean***'s support, a step-by-step plan appears behind him:*

> *Step 1. Buy drinks.*
>
> *Step 2. Discuss . . . drinks?*
>
> *Step 3. Express admiration at her resilience.*

A signal/gesture from **Jean***: 'Maybe something less intense.'* **Alan** *quickly rethinks the last step. Adjusts it to 'express casual admiration'. Feeling slightly more centred now, he finds himself . . .*

Scene Four: The Pub

. . . in the pub. **Craig** *comes to help with* **Alan***'s round.*

Craig Thanks, mate, this is perfect. Lot less intense than 'Oh, hey, let's just the two of us go down to the boozer'. (*Off* **Alan***'s look.*) Sorry, wingman duty isn't like messing up your commute or anything is it?

Alan Oh. No, I get the 140.

Craig Right down the road. *Ideal.* (*They reach the table.*) So Alannah, Alan here was telling me you used to do some sex work. And I was telling him that I think that's actually really fucking cool.

Alannah Yeah? Just today you found that out, was it?

Craig Hey, not all 'goss' walks its way up to my ivory tower, okay? Alan? Mate, do we keep you fully offline out of the office?

Alan Eh . . .

Alannah I've a question. For the table.

Craig Ooh. Fingers on buzzers.

Alannah   Who remembers the very first ticket they *had* to delete? Alan, why don't you start us off –

Craig *makes a 'wrong answer' buzzer noise.*

Craig   Eh, work talk. When me and Kofi were coming here – before he went cry-cry and hung up the lanyard – we made that the first commandment of Early House Humpday Crew. Thou shalt not discuss thine work or the ethics of thine work.

Alannah   Keep, delete, who gives a shit. Not asking about that, I'm – . . . (*Re-thinking.*) Let's say it's a bet. Because, me, I'm wagering that *you* can remember. Alan, original deletion.

Beat. **Alan** *feels the pressure.*

Alan   Eh . . . there was a dog being set on – . . . there were fireworks. I think.

Craig (*looking for the spotlight*)   Right. Well I can't remember the first, cos I'm not – you know. (*Gestures to* **Alan**.) *But* – from back when I was on your floor – the one I *tell* people about is the time I got a ball. Like, *a* testicle, singular. Some awareness ad. It'd make you think, you know. (*To* **Alannah**.) What about you? Remember your first?

Alannah   No. I'd say most people don't.

Craig   *Yeah.* Now can we maybe move away from . . . exploding doggos and work? (*Clutching.*) I mean . . . Sudan?

Alannah (*correctly suspecting he knows little*)   Yeah. Go on.

Craig   Just the . . . goings on. There. Like . . . proper Fubar. El loco.

Alannah (*moving it on*)   Well said –

Craig   I mean, if they *are* going on.

He looks around at them both.

Oh no . . . *No.* Don't tell me you yomp down your bowls of Newsios without even checking the nutritional side of the packet. The 'news'. (*Pronouncing 'noose'*.) The 'news' around our necks. What your *Mail*, or – I'm guessing – your *Guardian* tell us is all actually 'definitely happening'.

Alannah   You'd happily book a package holiday to anywhere in Sudan this weekend, would you?

Craig   I'm – look, I'm not saying there *isn't* a war. That's actually the last thing I'm saying, love. Sorry, do you mind that I called you love there? (*Not really awaiting a response*.) Look, I don't wanna get up on my soapbox about it –

Alannah   Swell, then I've another question for the –

Craig   Let me *just* – I've started so I'll finish, okay? The caps lock rants that come up on your screens. Jet fuel can't melt steel beams, Woody Harrelson's dad snipered JFK, my daughter joined a suicide pool and then half our village offed themselves, sure, majority of it is absolutely ravers. 99.9 per cent. But then, you know, sometimes with that *last* sliver of the pie chart . . . it can get a touch too clear why some people on high are so keen on getting those few posts gobbled on up. Scrubbed. (*Catching himself, wry*.) Ah. Look at me. Help me down off – give me a hand down off this soapbox, will ya? (*To* **Alannah**.) Look, my overall . . . *provocation* is that with Miss Midjourney, with Miss Information, can we really believe *anything* that pops up on those screens? I mean, could you name me one thing on your monitors that you can categorically, hand on heart, say was bona fide real?

Silence. **Craig** *hasn't twigged what he's said.*

Alan   Eh . . . Craig. Her brother – . . .

Craig   What? (*Finally clocking it*.) Oh. Sure. (*Trying to move it on*.) I'll eh – . . . get another round in. Samesies againsies?

Alannah   I'm going for a smoke. Alan?

Alannah *gets up and goes.*

Craig (*quietly to himself*)   Samesies againsies.

He goes to the bar. **Alan**, *alone, is unsure what to do. He re-checks his notebook. A lone step remains:*

   Step 3. Express casual admiration at her resilience.

Steeling himself, **Alan** *approaches* **Alannah**. *Silence. She offers him a cigarette.*

Alan   Oh, I don't eh . . .

Beat.

I *can* though . . .

Alannah (*decides to move it on*)   Do you remember the breed? (*Off his look.*) The dog. From that first ticket that you deleted.

Alan   Oh . . . it was a . . . one of those little eh – . . . A cocker spaniel.

Alannah (*to herself, relieved*)   Thank fucking Christ.

Beat. **Alan** *is unsure how to read this reaction.*

Alan   Do you – . . . you'd be quite *anti*-spaniel then?

Alannah   No, no – (*Getting to it.*) It's like a photographic memory you have, isn't it? That's what people – . . . I mean, maybe to you it seems normal.

Alan (*confused, polite*)   Sorry, I –

Alannah (*barrelling through*)   4 August. A Sunday. (*Takes out phone, scrolls.*) A video came onto your screen. Definitely your workstation, I checked the log today. This video arrived at 5.23 a.m. You had it deleted by 5.24 a.m. So it was a minute long tops. Came from the account 'LarryBakes'. Most likely would have been a one-person piece to camera. Male, white, early thirties. Blond. Maybe wearing a hoodie.

Alan   Eh, would you know the . . . subject matter of the –

Alannah   Laurence posted it. My brother. Right before the video of him dying. It was his second last communication ever. And it comes up as unavailable now. Cos you deleted it.

Beat.

Alan   Eh – . . . I wouldn't really remember too much from work that day –

Alannah   Yes but that's right now that you don't remember. But like you had to with that dog one, I need you to reach *right* back into the – that mental hard drive. 4 August –

Alan   I made up the dog one. With the fireworks. I thought it . . . was going to sound weird if I didn't remember that first one. I don't really remember any of them. Much. From *any* day.

Beat.

Alannah (*not accepting this*)   No. No. If anyone, *anyone* could remember, it'd be you. And you're the one who deleted it, so, yeah, it has to be you.

Alan   Sorry. Why do you think I could remember it?

Alannah   Because you're – you're fucking AA. That's what they call you, right?

Alan   . . . Accurate Alan?

Alannah   What? *No.* Alan Fucking Android.

Alan   Oh . . .

Alannah   Fuck. (*A lot louder.*) Fuck!

She knocks over a table in anger. Silence. After a moment, **Alan** *goes to right it.*

Alannah   Don't.

Alan   . . . okay.

Silence.

Alannah   I know it's still on some server somewhere. Tried to FOI it. Can't even do that. Because I'm not the account user. (*A breath.*) It's a *fucking* . . . suicide note being put through the wash. Again and a-fucking-gain. (*Fed up.*) I'm going to the bathroom.

As she goes to go, **Alan** *has another quick look in his notebook.*

Alan   I think it's admirable. (*She stops. Stares at him.*) What you're . . . doing. I think it's really admirable.

Alannah   . . . what?

Alan   I – . . . know you've things that can't be answered. I think they're the most difficult things to have. The questions. But you coming back to try to stop what happened to your brother happening to others. I think that's . . . yeah. Really . . . admirable. Sorry, keep using that same word over and over –

Alannah   Stop it happening to others?

Alan   Well . . . yeah. Like, when we remove the . . . footage. Those videos. Like Laurence's. It can prevent others going down the same – . . . (*Realising.*) Unless of course, you're mostly back to . . . find things out about your brother's post, which – . . . as I'm saying it, makes a lot more sense than –

Alannah   Can I ask you something? How long have you been removing footage with the aim of preventing more people from killing themselves?

Alan   Five years.

Alannah   They stopped yet?

Beat.

You didn't know why they called you AA? (*Off his look.*) Sorry about that.

She goes. **Alan** *looks in his notebook. A phrase jumps out from the opening illustration. 'I can help'. A little deflated, he looks at it. And then walks into . . .*

Scene Five: Home

. . . his room. At this desktop, **Alan** *hits search on: 'Alannah Baker'. He hits an option to 'Follow'. Then changes his mind. 'Unfollow'. Then back to 'Follow'. After a few quick rounds of this:*

Tina (*offstage*)   We decent, love?

Alan *quickly shuts the browser window.*

Alan   Yep. All good.

Tina *enters.*

Alan   Could you not . . . get back asleep?

Tina   New steroids get me so wired I need to do a bump of coke to wind down from them. (*Off his look.*) All good. Glad to meet the day.

Beat.

Speaking of meetings. Go on. Some new blood on the team, is it?

Alan   Yeah.

Tina   'Bout fucking time. Bad enough they make you field questions about tracker mortgages from Aussies all night, it's worse that they make you do it alongside people with the personality of bathroom carpet. Ask if you can do all your shifts next to the newbies. Honestly. A bank is a big old village. Redistribution is what they do. *I'll* ask them for you, if you want.

Alan   No, it's okay, I'll . . . I'll get on to them.

Tina   Good. (*Points at notebook.*) Big old world out there too.

Beat. **Alan** *picks up on* **Tina** *lingering a little.*

Alan   Are you – . . . do you maybe need something, Mum?

She sizes it up.

Tina   Maybe . . . (*Bites the bullet.*) Okay. *Okay.* So I caved. I bought the add-on option, the profile 'booster'. Only lasts for seven days though. Meaning I now need to dive headlong into operation 'Fuck It, Let's Give This Another Spin'. Know what I want from each shot, what I need is two – three minutes max of Photoshop time and – . . . do you mind?

Alan   Eh – . . . no, not really.

Tina   I'll take 'no, not really' to the bank. Okay.

A photo is shown to **Alan***. A photo of* **Tina** *in Brittas Bay.*

Me in Brittas. Can *just* about tolerate and it's . . . *semi*-recent.
But could do with being a smidge brighter. (*Seeing he's
elsewhere.*) Alan?

Alan   Yep, no, I can do that.

Tina   Great. Second. Calling this my 'not a social recluse'
photo. *But* I made the mistake of sitting next to Considerably
Better-Looking Deborah from Logistics. So I cropped her
out but her hand is still there

Another photo. A smiling **Tina** *sips a cocktail. Deborah's hand is on
her shoulder.*

So now it looks like I'm cavorting with Thing from the
Addams Family. Do you reckon you could disappear the
hand?

Alan   I *think* so . . . (*Clocking her expression.*) What?

Tina   There's a last one, that I just need a bit of . . . extra
support with.

Alan   Okay. Send it on to me.

*She takes off her dressing gown to reveal a dress underneath (same
one from the 'not a social recluse' photo). She quickly snaps a selfie
of the two of them.*

Tina   Sorry, you just never would have agreed to that.

Alan   Mum . . . No. You . . . can't put that up.

Tina   Okay. Can I maybe explain *why* I think it's important
to me to –

Alan (*tumbling out*)   *Mum*, people won't want to look at a
photo of your fucking . . . weirdo fucking Android son, okay.

Silence.

Tina   Love, did everything go okay in the pub this morning?

Alan   Yeah. They – . . . they messaged about doing it again. I'm just, sorry . . . I'm a bit tired. You can . . . put that one up, it's fine.

Tina   You sure? (*He nods.*) Just a proud mama, that's all.

Beat.

Alan   Mum, was there a reason why – . . . was there a rush to do this today?

Tina   Today?

Alan   Just with . . . anniversaries.

Tina   Oh. (*Genuine.*) No, love, I'm just working off Doctor Collins's timetable. And I feel like if I don't do it now, I'll – . . . No, I stopped letting your dad, letting that fucking man influence things a while ago. Full honesty, I actually don't think I even clocked the date.

Beat.

But you did though, which is fine –

Alan (*quelling the incoming question*)   You should – sorry for interrupting – you should have them now. The photos.

Tina   . . . Thanks. (*Seeing them.*) Oh. God . . . they look alright, don't they?

Alan   Is it not a bit weird that you're wearing the same dress in all but one of them? Looks a bit like you've been alive for a day.

Beat. **Tina** *considers the point. Scratches for a solution and then.*

Tina   Fuck it. (*Hits upload.*) And. We. Are. Live.

Beat.

(*Purposely flippant.*) Yeah, no bites, abject failure. Mind you, I haven't put the CF stuff in the bio yet. That'll fire some engines.

Alan   Oh. Is this an app geared at people with cystic fibrosis?

Tina   Oh, yeah, yeah. They let you select certain options, so if I want, I can tick the box that says I'm 'post-lung transplant', 'post-isolation'.

Alan   Really?

Tina   No, Alan, they would make no fucking money. It's Bumble.

Beat. She goes to leave. Stops. She turns her back on him.

Hey . . . which back has your back?

Alan   . . . Mum.

Tina   Which back?

Alan (*he indicates her back*)   . . . This back. Which . . . back has your back?

Tina *indicates that he needs to turn around.* **Alan**, *needing cajoling, does so.*

Tina (*indicating his back*)   This back.

She exits. **Alan** *re-opens the browser window. He sees something.* **Alannah**, *lit on stage, speaks it.*

Alannah (*speaking her status*)   Alannah Baker is online

Alan (*tentative, typing*)   Hey, about earlier, I just wanted to reach out –

Alannah (*speaking her status*)   Alannah Baker is offline

. . . **Alan** *stares at the monitor. And his unsent message.*

Scene Six: Work

A rush of images of content. A sped-up work-day. And then . . .

. . . **Alan**'s *in the break room. Looking at his phone again. The unsent* **Alannah** *message. He's still debating about whether to send it when . . .* **Georgina** *walks in. Tearful, she's come in to cry. But now sees he's there too.*

Georgina   Oh. Hi. You been . . . on yet today?

Alan   Yeah. (*Remembering.*) It's . . . Georgina, isn't it?

Georgina   Yeah. Alan, right? (*Can't stop herself.*) There was a – just now, there was a thing with a boy and a . . . cheese grater and – . . . Sorry, you've just done a whole – . . . You don't need to talk about it.

Beat. She lingers.

It's just . . . you know, you spend five minutes deciding whether someone getting called a stupid Welsh bitch is hate speech and then the next ticket is a – . . . It's really all a bit fucking . . . *beyond* isn't it?

Beat.

Alan   On the fifth floor, they – I think it's still the fifth – they have a – . . .

Georgina   Oh, Trevor? (*Off his nod.*) Yeah, they said about him. At the instructional.

Beat.

Thanks.

She exits. **Alan** *begins to draw. As he does, he becomes aware of* **Jean**'s *presence again.*

Alan   It's been on my mind a bit. The sequence of events that day. Laurence put up a post. I took it down. And it was only *then* that he did what he did. And I've been thinking, what if whatever he posted wasn't some inappropriate – wasn't *just* some inappropriate thing. What if it was

something of value. To him. His life's work or something.
What if me taking it down was the last bit of wind at his back
that he – . . . (*A breath.*) What if it didn't help this time?

*The drawing shifts. The phrase 'I Can Help' is now being
repeatedly scrawled. Eventually it's updated to: 'I Can Help
Someone'. It lands with* **Alan**.

On his phone, he flicks to **Laurence Baker**'*s page: LarryBakes.*

Alan   Right. So in order to help, we – Step One – we need
to know Mr Laurence Baker better. Need to distil his
interests.

*We see the total number of accounts LarryBakes was following: '2'.
And we see the accounts are: Lidl and SimOne.Says.*

Which he's . . . helpfully already done. Was following two
people. 'Simone Says' and Lidl. So we know, he was a . . . no-
frills consumer. And Simone is – . . .

Alan *clicks onto the SimOne.Says account. Their avatar profile is
a photo of black and white orbs. There are no posts on the account.
1,536 follow them. They follow no one. Their bio reads: 'Follow to
play.'*

Has no . . . posts. And likes . . . orbs. (*Looks to* **Jean**.) No, this
is progress . . . this was maybe like a community Laurence
was part of.

*He clicks into a list of SimOne.Says's followers. Many of whom
have the same white orbs as their profile pic.*

A community of orb . . . fanciers. Like . . . eh . . . Jeremy
here.

He clicks into **Jeremy**'*s account. A pinned post comes up.*

Jeremy (*speaking the post*)   It's with great sadness that we
announce the passing of Jeremy. He was loved and suffers
no more.

Alan, *thrown, clicks into the account of another SimOne.Says
follower:* **Maxine**.

Maxine (*speaking the post*)   Maxine is now no longer with us but as a digital monument to her we're –

Alan *hits the back button. He looks to* **Jean**. *A worried* **Jean** *gives a head shake.*

Alan   Eh . . .

He then clicks into multiple accounts. A smattering of memorial posts are heard. They aurally intermingle and build together.

Pranesh (*speaking the post*)   Pranesh, beloved son, leaves behind a –

Vinny (*speaking the post*)   So long everyone. This is not your fault. All my love – Vinny.

Paulo (*speaking the post*)   Never thought we'd be here. But it's my duty to –

Muriel (*speaking the post*)   This is Muriel, signing out. Peace. Peace to you all.

Virginia (*speaking the post*)   The above picture of Virgina was taken when she was just eight weeks old. Still feels incredible to us that she's no longer –

Kazuo (*speaking the post*)   Please don't mourn me. But please help my parents and partner get through this. – Kazuo

Lindy (*speaking the post*)   Lindy is gone. She thinks no one will notice. We disagree.

The sound builds and builds until . . . **Craig** *walks in. He clocks* **Alan**.

Craig   *Yes.* Listen, they're on my neck at the moment cos they think I short-staffed the day shift, which I definitely did *not.* So how does you fancy working a double? (*Off his hesitance.*) You'd be really helping me out, mate.

Alan   . . . Sure.

Craig   Attaboy. That's the AA, we know and love.

Alannah *enters.*

Craig   Ah. (*Winks to* **Alan**.) It's eh, Alannah, right?

Alannah (*no time for it*)   Yep, Alannah. I let you conduct oral sex on me last night because it was preferable to you continuing to talk and cry at me –

Craig   I'll let them know we got sorted.

He goes. As **Alannah** *gathers her things,* **Alan** *stares over at her. He considers it. Decides to say nothing. And then, a notification pops up. A post from SimOne.Says: 'Tonight's Contestant is 24 Forest G.'*

He stares at it. Then looks over at **Alannah**. *She eventually sees his look.*

Alannah   . . . What?

Scene Seven: Home

Alan *arrives home. He's a bag of nerves.* **Jean** *enters. Makes an attempt to calm* **Alan**.

Alan   Okay, okay. Blueprint for . . . *hosting* Alannah.

In his notebook, he makes a quick step-by-step checklist, ticking the steps as he goes:

Step 1. Ensure Mum is out for the night.

Step 2. Achieve and maintain calm.

Step 3. Look up witticisms in order to impress –

Alannah *walks in. Mid-list. He freezes. She looks at him.*

Alannah   Door was open.

Alan   Yeah, no it can . . . do that.

Alannah *moves it on. She's armed with post-it notes. Ready to create an 'investigation board'. She hands him a black marker.*

Alannah   Okay, *Zodiac*, *Seven*, Fincher vibes here we go.
The date the Sim One account started, when people were
first invited to 'play'. 12 May 2023.

Alan   . . . alright.

With a black marker, on a white background, she writes.
Uncomfortable, he stares.

Alannah (*oblivious to his discomfort*)   Number of current
followers: 1536. (*Reacting to it.*) What are you doing?

Alan   Just getting you a different . . . marker. That one's a
bit . . . faded.

He gives her a red marker, takes away the black one. She shrugs.
Writes up '1536'.

Alannah   And how many of them are now dead? (*Off his*
uncertainty.) Not asking you to reach in and yank the figure
from your arsehole, I'm about to tell you. It's fifty-nine. Fifty-
nine profile pictures of the weird fucking orbs, fifty-nine
farewell messages. And do you wanna guess how many
weeks have gone by since 12 May 2023? (*Off his non-guess.*)
Okay, you're bad at this. Fifty. *Nine.* So . . . Since May 2023,
this person, this account, on a weekly basis posts the address
of someone who follows them. Then gets them to end
themselves.

Alan   . . . 'end themselv–'

Alannah   And, *and* – whoosh, then they get it all to
disappear. (*Off his look.*) Right. Screenshot of the account
from earlier.

An image of the post comes up: 'Tonight's Contestant is 24 Forest
G.'

And now this is their current, live page.

The live SimOne.Says page comes up. No posts are listed.

Alannah   '24 Forest G.' Gone. Like spit in the rain. This Sim One motherfucker, they post it. Gets seen by all their followers. Then they hit delete.

Alan   But . . . why would this Simone person delete the record of –

Alannah   Firstly, Sim *One*. A *gut-twistingly*, tech bro-ingly clever pun on 'Simon Says'. And secondly, you are – I assume – *quite* familiar with your classic suicide message boards, your pro-mortalism forums, yes? (*Off his nod.*) So you know that there's always a trail of posts or how to instructions or . . . *whichever*. Enough smoking guns to get you the wrong side of the online safety act. With this, nada. A suicide pool free from moderation.

Alan   Okay. But is this not a bit of . . . guesswork? If names have been deleted, we can't *know* that they were ever put up in the first –

Alannah   *Again,* not names. Addresses. 24 Forest G equals 24 Forest Grove.

Alannah *writes out '24 Forest G'.*

In this fair rainheap, we have only a fistful of Forest G addresses. Three Forest Greens. One Forest Glen. Four Forest Groves. And only one goes up to 24. Forest Grove in Naas. Q, E – fucking – D. Might have been Gdansk last week for all we know. But tonight, it's the bright lights of Naas, baby. It's where I'm going. And I'm gonna need you to see it too.

Alan   . . . Oh? Not like . . . the police?

Alannah   Yeah, cos they'll understand this *too* much. They'll take it *too* seriously. Look, this is the first time this has resembled *any* level of sense. Fifty-nine people. One a week, on a weekly basis. *But* . . . there's no such thing as a pool with a hundred per cent follow-through rate – always people who opt out – so how could they *possibly* get this hit rate?

Alan   Do you – . . . I'm not sure if you want me to answer or not –

Alannah   Cos it's coerced. Made to look voluntary, but it ain't. Only way it works. Which makes even *further* sense when it comes to Laurence. Cos he – let me tell you – he was not some Heaven's Gate disciple waiting in line for his paper cup of Kool-Aid, okay.

Alan   But –

Alannah   Someone *forced* him to do this. Took it out of his hands.

Alan   Right. (*Tentative.*) And . . . how could they have done that?

Alannah   Dunno. A raised syringe behind the camera. Who knows –

Alan   To fifty-nine people . . . scattered all over the world on a weekly basis for the last –

Alannah   Maybe they have some dirt on them, some leverage.

Alan   Enough so that people, on a weekly basis, choose to die instead of –

Alannah   Stop saying 'weekly fucking basis', Alan. I know it's a weekly basis, I'm the one who fucking *determined* it was a weekly fucking basis. (*Regaining control.*) You think I'm being taken in by a hoax. Right? That's fine. Say it.

Alan   I – . . . accept that there were fifty-nine profiles of orbs but . . . do we know for certain they're not, like, bots? (*As she tries to respond.*) And to – . . . *briefly* continue on that point . . . if what you say happened, then why wasn't Laurence's profile also the orbs?

Alannah   Yeah, I'm ten fucking minutes into this thing, okay. Don't know *everything* yet. But you and I, after tonight, we fucking will. (*Seeing his reticence.*) Yes, you and I. Think about it, Alan. You've watched – what – ten thousand of these videos. You've probably seen the prick. If he's ever slid into frame or, whatever, if someone can ID him, it'd be you.

Alan   But if he's caught in the act how would me ID'ing him help?

Alannah   Okay, well, maybe it's more a case of –

Alan   And I did say that I don't really have a good recall for details and faces from the videos, so why would I be essential to –

Alannah   Because I fucking need someone else to care about this, how about that?

Silence.

Oh my God. How stupid, am I? Standing here. Thinking you get it. Thinking you've an . . . empathy chip that can –

Tina *enters. Hoovering. Headphones on. In her own world, she doesn't spot them initially. In both bewilderment (**Alannah**) and horror (**Alan**), they both watch her. A few beats. And then, **Tina** clocks them. A stunned silence. She removes her headphones. And then.*

Tina   . . . Good evening.

Alannah   Bathroom upstairs?

Alan *nods.* **Alannah** *goes.*

Alan   I – . . . thought you were at outpatients.

Tina   They said it'll be a shorter wait tomorrow for a level check. (*Gesturing.*) Who –

Alan   She's eh . . . from work. She's – . . . her name's Alannah.

Beat.

Tina   I've decided I'm handling this with nuance and aplomb.

Alannah *re-enters.*

Tina   Hi. I'm Tina. Alan's eh . . . I live in Alan's.

Alannah   Okay. I'm Alann–

Tina (*a little too late with it*)   Francesca, is it?

Alannah   Alannah.

Tina   *Alannah.* Lovely to accidentally meet you, Alannah.

As she goes to leave, her phone pings. Checking the notification, she stops at the door and turns.

I'm – . . . I *will* be gone in a second. But can I just clarify . . . a superswipe is . . .?

Alannah   . . . Bumble? (*Off her nod.*) It's when someone really likes your profile. You can only give out a few a week.

Tina (*reassured, excited*)   Right, that's what I'd – . . . Thanks.

Making to leave, she checks the profile. Stops in her tracks again.

Quick little follow-up question. Is that, like, a lighting thing or is there not a great deal of . . . facial symmetry on show there?

She tentatively shows the phone to **Alannah**.

Alannah   Oh. (*Checking it.*) Eh . . . yeah, think you can chuck that particular fish back.

Tina   Wow, he – I know you didn't mean it – with the chin he actually does sort of look a bit like –

Alannah   No, my words were considered there. (*Seeing it, embarrassed.*) You know you just – . . . did you mean to match with him?

Tina   Gonna keep him as a maybe. Even if us watching *The Shape of Water* together could be uncomfortably autobiographical. (*Off* **Alan**'s *'please leave' look.*) Anyway, look who's oversharing and still here.

Alannah   . . . I think I know him.

Tina   Oh. Okay.

Alannah   He was a – let me just *double* check (*Looks at it.*) –
Actually, no. I thought he had a – . . . My guy had a neck
tattoo. I thought he was a former subscriber.

Tina   Oh. Podcast?

Alannah   No. I . . . used to do a bit of 'camgirl' work. While
back. Do you . . . It's fine if you don't know what that is.

Tina   Oh . . . yeah, no, I know what it is.

Alannah   Okay. (*Expanding.*) I'm not, like, embarrassed by it
or anything. Can't stay in the one lane forever. It offered
more dosh than Costa Coffee and you had to talk to people a
lot less. That was actually – in the end – that was the buzzkill.
Regulars, like him, they'd start *sharing* in the chat. *Life* stuff,
'my mother fell' stuff. Since then I've been temp-girl, paint
mixer-woman, switchboard-lady. But guess which one they
just *love* to chat about at work.

Tina   Ha. Right.

Alannah   (*misreading her laugh*)   Okay. You're uncomfortable.
I'm making you both uncomfortable. I've been told I 'do
that'. I'll go – I'll shut up. And you can both be as . . .
'sympathetically' judgemental as you like. It's fine. I –

Tina   Who was judging you exactly?

Alannah   . . . Well, you get to know 'the look'. So I –

Tina   Okay, 'assume' what you want about me. But
definitely do not assume he is. My son has never judged
anyone in his waking life. To his detriment at times. And for
the record, why would *I* care what you do on there? You do
you, okay. (*Off* **Alan**'s *look.*) I've been *trying* to fucking leave.

Alannah   Well, I'm – . . . actually not really *on* there as
much anymore. It's something they do. With the older
content. Wasn't worth the bandwidth. Lol.

Tina   Oh. How'd it get out in work then?

Alannah (*uncomfortable, caught out*)   . . . Yeah. Dunno.

Beat. As **Tina** *clocks that* **Alannah** *was the one who told, she takes mercy and moves it on.*

Tina   Well, no offence, but it all still sounds like more fun than the bank.

Alannah   The – . . . what, sorry?

She looks to **Alan**. *She realises the lie instantly. Silence.* **Tina** *spots the look.*

Tina   What? Have I put a foot in my mouth here? Do you love the bank?

Alannah   . . . Yeah. The stability's nice. (*Gestures to the post-its.*) We're planning a heist actually.

Tina   Right. (*Sensing the moment.*) Well, I'll leave you to, eh – . . . *this*. Good to meet you, Alannah.

She goes. **Alan** *looks at* **Alannah**. *He wants to make a case for going with her. As he goes to speak:*

Alannah   24 Forest Grove, are you in or are you –

Alan (*saying it too quickly*)   Yes.

Scene Eight: Stakeout

Alan *is now sat in the car. Alone. They're parked outside 24 Forest Grove. In his notebook, he doodles the outline of their car.* **Alannah** *re-enters. She comes to the door of the car.*

Alannah (*impatient*)   Door? (*He unlocks it, she gets in.*) Yep. No lights on in the back as well. No one home in 24 Forest G. Whatever death cult this is, whatever pentagrams they want to daub on the ceiling, they're not here yet.

Alan   There could always be people upstairs. Gone to bed early.

Alannah   Upstairs was empty too. (*Off his look.*) Key was under the flowerpot.

Beat.

This ain't no hoax. Someone is coming and something fucking big is about to happen. Can just – . . . I know it. (*Looking to him.*) Did you not get a sandwich at the petrol station? (*He shakes his head.*) Have you seen like, *zero*, stakeout films?

Silence.

So what, she thinks you've been managing tracker mortgages for the last five years?

Alan   I don't think she'd . . . *love* to know what it is I'm doing.

Alannah   And why *do* you do it? And – since I'm asking – why are you not, like, a manager by now? Why are you *still* on the self-harm queue?

Beat.

Thanks for that unblinking, non-answer. Feel *very* at ease now. (*Thinking of it.*) Oh. Maybe I should take down the licence plates in case we –

She grabs his notebook. It opens on a page, a chaotic beachhead. It's briefly projected. **Alan** *hurriedly grabs it back. Shuts it.*

What the fuck . . .? Alan, what the shit was that.

Alan   It's just a – . . . I doodle.

Alannah   Yeah. *Before* you put the lotion on its skin or *after* it gets the hose again or. What is that serial killer shit?

Alan   It was something I was doing about . . . work.

Alannah   Alan. (*No response.*) You are aware that I work with you. *That* is not what we do. (*No response.*) Alan . . .? *Alan?* Can't thousand-yard stare your way out of this one, okay –

Alan, *no other way out, opens the notebook. He talks through each part of the drawing.*

Alan The first bit is – that's the news interviewing me. I don't know why the news is interviewing *me*. But they ask me why it's important. The work. And . . . I ask them to imagine a beachhead. To imagine this massive wave hitting it. And – the wave – it belches out tonnes of plastic and rubbish from the ocean – stuff that *we've* put there – all out onto this beachhead. And then there's us, the people to clean it up. Some days you might only get it half-tidied, you might *just* be finishing when a new day's wave dumps a whole new lot of it out on the sand. So, you have to start again. Green bottle by green bottle. Syringe by syringe. And that might seem pointless. But people forget . . . the sea life you've saved, the things you've saved that day by doing it. The seagull that never got caught in a ring pull cos you picked it up. Maybe that's you taking down a post that could've made some kid do something that . . . means the world doesn't get to have that kid anymore. And if you're a manager, you do it a lot less. That part. And I think it has – that that has value. I actually say that to the news interviewer. That last bit. And that's sort of . . . it. They cut to the weather then.

Silence.

Alannah I actually didn't know you could talk that much.

Alan And I'm sorry about the water thing. That time.

Alannah . . . what?

Alan That day in the break room. After you'd . . . seen what you'd seen. And I . . . I just said that you should keep drinking water. Cos I know . . . in situations like that, people can forget to do it.

Silence.

Alannah Okay. I've just seen the video again. Select your words. Go for it.

Silence.

Yeah, isn't a shitload *to* say, is there? I saw what I saw.

Alan   I wish I'd seen it instead.

Silence. **Alannah** *swaps around the sandwich halves. She takes the smushed one. She thinks she sees someone going into the house.*

Alannah   Oh.

Alan   Think it's just someone walking their dog.

Alannah   . . . What a prick

Beat.

You go into Trevor much? I mean, I know you do your (*Points at notebook.*) . . . Art attack, therapy thing. But like that . . . that's only gonna get you so far, right?

Alan   . . . Right.

Alannah   As part of their 'please, please, don't go to the broadsheets with your trauma' package, they said I could have continued access to Trevor. And if you *do* go into him, them guts you see all over the wall? Mine own. Cos I'm fucking *ace* at therapy. Therapy *anorak.*

Beat.

He told me this story – think he'd heard it on a podcast or something – about a telemarketer. In Montreal. A temp job to him. And with the way the job worked, with the machine, his phone is always autodialling. Constantly. Nine to five. The second you ended your conversation, the *second* they refused to buy ink toner from you or whatever, it'd start dialling someone else. Meaning the only lull you'd have is when you'd get someone's answering machine. You could breathe for those thirty seconds as some bint told you they weren't 'in right now'. And mid-way through year ten of this, mid-way through a random shift on some random Tuesday, our guy ends some random call. His computer autodials. And after a ring or two, he hears the sound of an answering machine clicking into gear. He relaxes back into the chair, ready to enjoy his mini-break. And then . . . he sits up. Cos he's hearing his own voice back at him. His *own* answering machine explain to himself that he can't take his own call because he's out at the moment. At the same temporary job he's worked in for ten years now.

Beat.

The population of the Montreal metropolitan area is four million.

Beat.

Trevor's point was – I think – that, sometimes, you just get your own number.

Silence.

Silence works okay for you, doesn't it? (*Off his lack of reply.*) Fab.

She starts looking at her phone. **Alan** *stares straight ahead. Then returns to doodling in his notebook.*

Behind them, his earlier drawing completes. The car. With two kangaroos sitting up front. A bored **Alannah**, *unaware of any of this and lit by her phone screen, begins to nod off.*

A jarring black and white image strobes onto the screen.

It's morning now . . . **Alan** *is sat up, wide awake.* **Alannah** *is asleep. He tries to figure out a way to gently rouse her. Rolls down the window. Nothing. Turns on the air con. Nothing. He flicks the car light on and off. Nothing. As he goes to do something else . . .*

Alannah   Please stop everything you're doing.

Alan   Sorry.

She opens her eyes.

Alannah   Fuck. Did you stay awake?

Alan   I did.

Alannah   Anything? (*He shakes his head.*) Any more posts from Sim One? (*Another shake of the head.*) Right.

Alan   . . . I'm sorry.

Alannah   Why you sorry? I'm gonna go to Laurence's place. Check his laptop, his phone. See if Sim One ever contacted him. Or if there were ever any messages about Forest G or Whichever.

Alan   You haven't had a look in his place yet?

They begin driving off. She brandishes her phone at him.

Alannah   Stick the address in your phone, will you? Mine's dying. (*Seeing his aged smartphone.*) Sorry. *Sorry.* Does that retain exactly one kilobyte at a time? Do you let yourself have *any* nice things?

Alan   No, it's fine – . . . If I need to, I clear space as I go.

Alannah (*gestures at notebook*)   Well, I suppose those friends don't text, do they?

She clearly regrets what she's said. But doesn't know how to mend fences.

Alan   Do you've the address?

Alannah   35 Northbrook Avenue. (*Responding to him doing the task.*) Thanks.

Beat.

Alan   Can I raise a . . . thing?

Alannah   *God.* Yes. Roving permission to speak.

Alan   Is there a possibility that . . . Laurence just did it. You know. Unilaterally.

Alannah   Yeah, no, fairly certain I'd fucking know. My twin.

Beat.

What? What does that look mean?

Alan   Eh . . . well . . . (*Feels he has to say it.*) You . . . weren't friends. Online. Because – you know this – but if you're in someone's friends list or they're friends of friends, you don't get tickets from that account. But you got his video.

Beat. She slows down the car.

Alannah   Sorry. Are you implying that cos we weren't Bebo besties that I don't know my brother from a fucking hole in the ground.

Alan   No, I – . . . I didn't mean it like that. *Can* you . . . stop here?

Alannah   We're slowing not stopped and what fucking way *did* you mean it then?

Alan   Well . . . if you want to find out what happened, you sort of need to step by step it. And first step, would be to only go off concrete . . . *facts*. Cos otherwise, well, that's the type of thing that might lead us down – you down a good few blind alleys. And eh –

Alannah (*a torrent*)   His blood type was O negative, mine was B positive, unusual for twins to have different ones. He got 465 in the leaving, I got 390. He sang soprano in the choir with me until he was thirteen when his voice cracked. He trained for three marathons in college, completed two. And he had a phobia of hexagonal shapes but still liked the *taste* of honeycomb ice cream.

Alan   Okay. But isn't that all stuff from a while ago? From growing up in the same house?

Beat. She stops the car.

Alannah   Yeah, here's good for you I think, isn't it? Think there's a blind alley *just* here that's really fucking good for you actually.

Alan   I – . . . actually?

She opens his door. **Alan** *gets out of the car. She drives on.* **Alan** *is left there. She comes back. Chucks his notebook back out at him.*

Alannah   Take your fucking colouring book.

She drives off. **Alan** *is left waiting there.*

Scene Nine: Hospital

Alan *sits with* **Tina**. *They're in a consultant's office in the hospital. Waiting.*

Alan   Really sorry again about –

Tina   No apologies, love. Never had the rush of collecting someone from a hard shoulder before. I'm just sorry that you have to come to this snoozefest now. Well, that is if the lazy bastard ever shows up –

Mid-sentence, **Dr Collins** *appears.*

Tina   Ah! Dr Collins. If it isn't the chest doctor who's the best doctor.

Dr Collins   Morning, Ms Kenedy.

Tina (*to* **Alan**, *not quiet*)   Favourite patient. You go on, love, I'll be done in a bit.

Dr Collins   So sorry about this but I'm having some . . . technical issues. I'd like to show you your file but my desktop is frozen. Can't access the internal database.

Tina   The one day I didn't bring my back-up internal database.

The conversation falls into dumbshow. We're focused entirely on **Alan** *and his phone now. His thread with* **Alannah** *is open. He tries to compose a message . . .*

Alan (*speaking his messages*)   Hey, I'm sorry that I suggested that you and your brother weren't

He stops. Deletes. Starts again.

Alan   Hey, would it be possible to talk later? I think I misrepresented myself

He stops. Deletes. Starts again.

Alan   Hey, home safe?

He stops. Deletes. Tries to start again. A spotlit **Alannah** *appears.*

Alannah (*speaking her message*)   Can see you typing. Stop.

Alannah *goes.* **Alan** *looks at his phone. Pockets it. The rest of the room comes back into focus.*

Tina   Alan can help you out. (*To* **Dr Collins**.) He does computer stuff.

Alan   What, sorry?

Dr Collins   This is an *official* hospital console, I don't know that –

Tina   Sure, no, we'll all just hang on until the one lady in IT decides to send herself down.

Alan   I can have a . . . quick look if you like.

Beat. **Dr Collins**, *unsure, allows* **Alan** *to have a go at the desktop.*

Tina (*checking phone, a glimpse of frustration*)   Fuck sake, little fishy, take the hint. (*Realising* **Dr Collins** *heard*.) We're giving dating another go. Post-surgery, inspirational zest for life, etcetera. And I'm trying to chuck someone back overboard.

The computer screen unfreezes. It displays **Tina**'s *file. A small section of it is blown up:*

'TINA KENEDY – POST-TRANSPLANT – STAGE 4 – ACUTE RENAL FAILURE – KIDNEY AT 23% FUNCTIONALITY.'

Alan *and* **Tina** *stare at the screen. Silence.*

Tina   Whose is – . . . what's that?

Collins   . . . It's no cause for panic. New lungs are healthy. But we knew, post-transplant, immunosuppressants would

take a toll on the kidneys, and, eh . . . even there, a change
in meds could have a significant –

Tina   It's, eh . . . it's okay. We just, eh . . . come up with a
plan of attack, don't we?

Soon the room dissolves. It's just **Alan**. *The black and white letters
remain.*

Jean *arrives out.* **Alan** *closes his eyes. Tries to concentrate. The
letters on the screen begin to shift. They begin to make up the edges
of a familiar shape. The kangaroo. But at a certain point, they stop
moving. It all just breaks apart. And snaps back into:*

*'TINA KENEDY – POST-TRANSPLANT – STAGE 4 – ACUTE
RENAL FAILURE – KIDNEY AT 23% FUNCTIONALITY.'*

In a fit of anger, **Alan** *throws away/destroys the notebook.* **Jean**
suddenly disappears. A little alarmed, **Alan** *flinches. And then . . .
he convinces himself he's done right.*

Scene Ten: Work

. . . **Alan** *finds himself back at his desk. He stares into space.*
Alannah *is just across the way. With a drunken little stumble,*
Craig *enters. He's holding a can of beer.*

Craig   If isn't Android – . . . sorry, *AA*. Best trod the party
line . . .

Beat. He indicates **Alan**'s *screen.*

Craig   Doing a go-slow, are we? Don't feel like trying to
scoop up the buttshit of the world with a fucking teaspoon
today, huh? (*Off his look.*) Sorry. I'm just . . . we fucking
dump toxic waste downstream. Kick it down the river. And
expect it *not* to salmon its way back up at us.

Alannah   Craig, you wanna maybe bring the can outside –

Craig   Shut up, tramp. Okay. Zip it. They're sending *Trevor* down – *Uncle* Trevor to break the news to the rest of them. But until then, you're stuck with me alright.

Alannah   What news?

Craig   . . . 'Foot in the tech door.' Like, they'd bargepole any of us after we've seen what they keep in the basement. Twenty-four years old. Twenty-four years old. What's the – . . . what's the fucking point of a fucking point . . . .?

Alan   Craig. What's going on?

Beat.

Craig   You don't know? (*Off* **Alan***'s look.*) Georgina. They found her in a toilet cubicle in a Burger King. Right after she finished here yesterday, she went there. That's where she fucking did it . . .

Alan   Did what?

Craig *looks to him.*

Craig   Fucking twenty-four years old. Headstone is gonna read Forest, Georgina. Twenty-four years old. That's what it's going to fucking say.

Beat. **Alan** *and* **Alannah** *look to each other.* '24, Forest G'.

Craig   Twenty-four years, did nothing. What are ours going to say? Did nothing, took longer to get there. This . . . fucking place.

Alannah *stares at* **Alan**. **Alan** *now just stares straight ahead.*

Lights.

Act Two

Scene One: Home

Alan *walks out on stage. He sets up a tripod. Places his phone on it. Hits record.*

Alan   . . . Cleared a fair bit of phone storage for this, so hopefully it . . . (*Getting back to it.*) When it was suggested there should be a chronicling of the Sim One investigation. Alannah thought podcast. And I thought what could be more helpful would be like . . . a filmed instructional. That we could post online. A 'how to' for anyone else interested in getting involved. I asked her if she'd be in front of the camera and she said, 'No, because I don't think your idea is good.' So . . . (*A 'here we are' gesture.*) This all feels . . . less juvenile though. More sophisticated. More refined. Which is really . . . good actually – This is very back foot, need to start now.

He presses a clicker. A heading comes up: Step One – Observe. After the main heading, he clicks through different slides as they come up (e.g. each of the SimOne.Says posts).

Alan   After Georgina, more names came in. New one each week. An IVF consultant from Bangalore. A food truck worker in Oregon. Bus driver in Khartoum. All different wage brackets. No pattern to it. All a hundred per cent follow-through rate. Which just . . . *shouldn't* exist. It also wasn't the only thing the account posted. For each name, they'd then put up a link to their funeral. A watch-along. They never responded to DMs. Before he died, Laurence had wiped his laptop. Meaning there was no record of correspondence from the account to him, so no way of getting their IP address and – what's more – no smoking gun. No message to show how he'd gotten Laurence or any of them to do it. No hard evidence of coercion. Meaning any attempts to report the account, bring it to the authorities, were – at best – ignored. But Georgina . . . we *knew* the account had contacted her too. So a plan was formed. And I thought – first up – we'd have to address our . . . *conflict*. But Alannah just wanted to get the team back together. To catch Simone.

Alannah (*arriving*)   Sim *One* dipshit. I'm going to Georgina's home. See if there was anything from him in her inbox.

Alan   Want me to come with? (*No response. Back out.*) . . . And so 'Team Alanannah' set out.

Alan *presses a clicker. A new heading comes up: Step Two – Field Research.*

Alannah   I'll talk. You just follow my lead. And don't say anything.

Alan (*polite confusion*)   How is that . . . following your lead –

Tristan, *the brother of* **Georgina**, *opens their front door.*

Alannah   Evening. Georgina Forest was once a resident here, yes? (*Off his look.*) Sorry, my name is Alannah. This is Alan. We work for – (*Company name *bleeped out**) who are, primarily, a third-party moderation service client for – (**Bleep**). We're calling around to –

Tristan   Bit late to be reaching out with condolences, isn't it?

Alan   We didn't . . . reach out to you?

Alannah (*a daggers look to* **Alan**)   *Big* oversight. Thing is . . . Georgina had a company laptop. And, as such, it has proprietary data. This is a horrible situation, I know, but –

Tristan   My mum is inside. She hasn't gotten out of bed for three weeks. I don't want her to hear this. If I give you the laptop will you just fuck off?

Alannah   *Permanently.*

Tristan *disappears back inside the house.* **Alannah** *turns to* **Alan.**

Alannah   So you have to be left in the car? That's now an established fact, is it?

Alan   Alannah, you gave our actual names and (*Bleep*)'s and (*Bleep*)'s name.

Alannah   *Relax.* We get her laptop to my guy, he can unlock *any* password, *any* firewall, so all her message history, anything from Sim can be –

CRASH. A laptop, thrown from the top window, lands on stage. It smashes in half.

Tristan   Anything else I can get for you?

Alan *presses a clicker. A new slide: Step Three – Profiling.*

Alan   As we'd nothing truly tangible, this process was a bit speculative. There seemed to be any number of archetypes that Sim could be.

Clicked-through phrases: 'Dissatisfied Father of Three'; 'Closet Incel'; 'Neo-Con Conspiracist'; 'Kremlin Hacker'; 'Extreme Porn Fancier'; 'Ex-Military PTSD vibes'.

But the sole motivation that Alannah assigned to him . . . that probably – . . . could have been more speculative.

One sole motive joins the screen: 'Wasn't Held as Child.'

Alan   The next 'contestant' was a park employee in Beirut. Then an Uber driver in Naples. But then . . . there was a dry cleaner. In Donegal. Whose phone or laptop could hold either some threat or instruction from Sim One. So –

Alannah (*arriving in, seeing it*)   Wait, did you . . . *print* your bus ticket?

Alan (*to* **Alannah**)   Yeah, my phone . . . sometimes overheats with PDFs.

Alannah   . . . You experience humiliation over all the wrong things.

He presses a clicker. A new slide: Step Four – BETTER Field Research.

Alan   In Donegal, the dry cleaner, his dad, was already back at work in the family shop.

Dry Cleaner *appears.*

Alan   And this time she said we were with –

Alannah   An unnamed cyber-security firm. We have reason to believe your son's devices are being posthumously hacked.

Alan (*out*)   Which, again, doesn't make a lick of sense.

Dry Cleaner   Not my problem, love. He topped himself at midnight. Stuck everything he owned up on Adverts at noon. All gonezo.

Alannah   *Everything?*

Dry Cleaner   Whole job lot. Now either gimme some trousers to press or fuck off.

Alan   Relatively quickly, we found the people who'd bought the phone and laptop. Alannah offered them both double what they'd just paid. And cos we had to get our bus back, she advised that we divide and conquer. The laptop. That was in a flat in Donegal Town. She went there. And, for the phone, I went to an estate just outside the town.

Alan *knocks on a door. A gruff man,* **Ollie***, answers it.*

Ollie   Locked iPhone? (*Off* **Alan***'s nod.*) Cash? (**Alan** *gives it.*) Bye.

Ollie *chucks the phone to* **Alan** *and goes.*

Alan   But on my way back into town. Something funny happened. Well, shouldn't say funny, minor theft is never funny. These two guys came up to me. When they saw my phone, they – they actually didn't want it. Then they got a look at the other one, the phone I'd just bought. Until that point I don't think I'd realised it. How important it was all becoming to me. Cos when they asked, I . . . wouldn't let the phone go from my grip. Well . . . again, probably shouldn't say 'asked'.

He clicks. A new slide. A photo of a bloodied **Alan***.*

The laptop guy, he ghosted us. But we'd the dry cleaner's phone. And all we needed to do was get it into the hands of her 'unlocking guy' . . .

A laptop repair shop. **Repair Person** *holds the phone.*

Repair Person   Nada. No messages. Hidden or otherwise from a . . . 'Sim One'.

Alannah   No, no, no, no there *is*. Some fucking – revenge-porn threat, some family hostage picture. *They* are *there*. Check again.

Repair Person   Scroll to your heart's content, love. Your phone now.

Repair Person *goes.*

Alan   That's when the final stage idea was born. A . . . joint effort.

Alannah   Those funerals. The ones he posts. There's gotta be something, some hint, some fucking detail in them, some way to catch him. We need to be watching all of them. But it's *not* going to be morbid or weird. Cos I'm bringing microwave popcorn.

Alan *presses the clicker. A new slide: Step One (but now also Step Five) – Observe.*

A montage. **Alan** *and* **Alannah** *watch a monitor and share popcorn. The names of each (e.g. 45 Tommasi B; 32 Curry L; 34 Nowak K; 24 Nkosi P) are projected for each. For every funeral change, we should hear a microwave ping.*

– We hear the sounds of an Italian funeral. They watch. She hogs the popcorn. Change to:

*– Sounds of an Australian funeral. She still hogs the popcorn.
Change to:*

*– Sounds of a Polish funeral. She offers him a little popcorn.
Change to:*

– Sounds of a South African funeral. The bowl sits between them.

Alan   Yet to bear fruit. But some fruit takes a while to . . .
bloom.

His alarm goes on his phone.

Right. I better . . . First shift back in a while. They – after
Georgina – they got us to take unused holidays. But . . . keep
watching for . . . the things.

He ends the video.

(*To himself.*) Need to workshop a sign-off.

A knock on the door.

Tina   Love, if you're talking to me I can't hear you. We have
walls.

Alan   No, I wasn't – . . . I was just on the phone. You can
come in.

She does so.

Tina   On the phone to whom exactly? (*Off his discomfort.*)
Okay, question retracted. Anyway, can spin you in if you like.

Alan   It's okay, I'm – . . . finishing up something here.
Where you going?

Tina   Oh. Doctor Collins has *deigned* to clear some time for
me. (*Off his look.*) I reckon it's good news. Probably only
doing it in person cos he wants a victory lap.

Alan   . . . Okay.

Beat.

Tina   Well, best of luck today, hope the return's not too – (*Noticing the absent notebook.*) Hey, you forgetting your Pocket Rocket?

Alan   Oh. It eh – . . . yeah, it ran out.

Tina, *slightly unsure about this, gives a warm nod. She goes.* **Alan**, *now more on edge, looks to his phone. Puts headphones back on.*

Alan   Let's just watch that back. (*After getting through two seconds of watching himself, he yanks off his headphones.*) Okay, podcast it is.

Scene Two: Work

Alan *arrives in to work. As he goes to put his phone away, he gets a message from* **Alannah**.

Alannah (*speaking the message*)   We've the Arizona funeral tonight. Happy crappy first day back.

Alan *turns on his workstation. 'Thank You for Making the Internet Safer'. A deep breath. Then . . . he goes to work. Meanwhile, as he works:*

. . . **Alannah** *is in* **Trevor**'s *office. A small therapy room in the main company building.*

Alannah   Fucking 'Alannah Allsorts'. Did I ever – Trevor, did I ever tell you that's what they used to call me? 'Alannah Allsorts'. Except – crucial detail – when *Dad* said it, it was meant in, like, a nice way. Because I'd always 'give it all a go'. Every sport, every . . . friend. But Mum, she liked it for a different reason. Never said as much, but I know she did. As a monument to my lack of staying power. You know. When it gets a bit . . . *dicey*. As though, you know, you should just – every job, every relationship – you should *welcome* a bad situation. *Live* in it permanently. I mean . . . she'd fucking know.

Beat. She's clocked that **Trevor***'s checked his watch.*

Alannah   You'd like to talk about something, Trevor?

Trevor   Oh. No. You never have to worry about what *I* want
to –

Alannah   Wouldn't be checking to see how long we have left
if you didn't want to bring something up.

Beat.

Trevor   I wanted to check in on how you're doing since
Georgina's passing. And – this is *me* asking, not . . . (*'the
company.'*) As we said at the time, it was likely something that
could have difficult . . . echoes for you. Namely, the anguish
you'd have felt missing Laurence's calls that day.

Alannah   Which day?

Trevor   The day he . . . passed. He – if I'm recalling
correctly – he'd been calling you but you couldn't get your
phone out of your locker.

Alannah   No. I was trying to get my phone out to call *him.*
But it was too late.

Trevor   Oh. I've misremembered that maybe. Sorry. So he
hadn't – . . . there hadn't been an attempt from him to
contact you that day?

Silence. He tries to claw it back.

Well, regardless of who contacted whom, I know that it must
have –

Alannah   You said it was okay, didn't you? If we finish up
early sometimes.

Lights down. We move back to . . .

Alan *finishes his workday. As he does, he's confronted with the
usual image. A black and white piece of pixelated content. The toll
of the day. He stares at it. Briefly feels the lack of* **Jean** *and the
notebook. And then . . . he swipes left. The image just . . . goes.*

Relieved, he takes a breath. That wasn't so bad. Vindication for ditching **Jean***.*

Scene Three: Break Room

As **Alan** *waits for her,* **Alannah***, still in a bit of a daze from her session, wanders in.*

Alan Hey, had you any further thoughts on that podcast idea, cos I don't know if – . . . well, I don't know if content *creation* is my strength.

Alannah No.

Alan Right. Well, we'll put a pin in that. (*Moving it on.*) So, I decided to group everyone. By careers. To see if there's a commonality, like even a distant one. And we now have – alphabetically – one anaesthesiologist. One cabin crew member. One content moderator. One dry cleaner –

Alannah Two content moderators. (*Off his confusion.*) Laurence. He did it. Few years back.

Alan Oh. Okay. Well, something will . . . shake loose. Has to. (*Picking up on it.*) You alright?

Alannah Yeah. Fine. Why.

Alan Eh . . . So for the IT guy from Arizona tonight. I found a, like, slightly *less* carcinogenic popcorn that we can –

Alannah Yeah, I'm gonna give that a miss, I think. Have a date.

Alan Oh. Alright. (*Keeping spirits up.*) Well, I'll have a full report on your desk by . . . close of day.

Alannah *goes.* **Alan** *lingers for a moment. Some hues of the negative pixelated colours creep in for a second. And then . . . the scene shifts.*

Scene Four: Home

Alannah *enters* **Laurence**'s *house. The tripod that he set up to film himself is still there. His black hoodie is still hung up on a hook.* **Alannah**, *silent, sits in the room. Takes it in. A feeling of coming to a decision about something.*

. . . Meanwhile, **Alan** *is in his own room. As he watches it on his laptop, we hear the sounds of the eulogy from Arizona:*

Eulogiser   Of course losing Anne-Marie in this way, by her own hand, is something that will be particularly difficult for our family to overcome. To speak plainly, it brings us right back to the time when we lost Anne-Marie's father, Michael. In much the same circumstances –

Almost involuntarily, **Alan** *shuts the laptop. He struggles to gather himself. Tries to suppress a sudden burst of panic. There's a knock on the door. He waits. And then . . .*

Alan   Yep. All good.

Tina *enters.*

Tina   Burning the midnight oil, are we?

Alan   Yeah, just, eh – . . . doing a little overtime.

Tina   Right. Just make sure it's on your terms, love. Not theirs. (*Sensing his uncertainty.*) Oh, sorry, I'm not trying to build suspense. Was sometimes hard to hear Doctor Collins with the sound of him patting himself on the back but it's positive news. His alternate meds plan, it's improving functionality. All trending upwards.

Alan   Right. Well, that's . . . that's great, Mum.

Tina   Hey, lest you forget, you're looking at Tina fucking – . . . what's the superhero film with Tina Turner?

Alan   Eh . . . she was in the second *Max Max* film?

Tina   Right. Well, if she makes it to the end of the film, that's me right there.

Beat.

Anyway, main headline I wanted to tell you is that the house is free this Saturday night. (*Off his look.*) I've a date. The 'Creature from the Black Lagoon'. Or 'Graham'. I decided to just – . . . Could be a laugh. And I don't need you to do anything. Except maybe . . . wish me a bit of luck before I go. Anyway, free gaff in case you and a certain person wanted more . . . privacy. And I'll say no more.

Alan   Mum, me and Alannah aren't – . . . it's not like that.

Tina   Well, that's fine too. I only want you to – . . . maybe you've felt a bit restricted by me. More than you should. And I just want you to –

Alan   More than I should?

Tina   Well, love, it's only one of us who's needed to hide away from the world.

Silence.

Okay. Love, I didn't – . . . mean to sound like your dad. I just – . . . why not grab this chance. Both hands. That's all.

Beat.

Hey, which back –

Alan   You know we don't – . . . We probably both – if we're being honest – we probably both feel a bit silly doing that. At this stage. So we don't have to keep – . . . Okay.

Beat.

Tina   Okay.

Beat. **Tina**, *no other choice, exits.* **Alan** *sits alone. Again, some of the 'bad content' colours infiltrate the scene. The funeral sounds bleed into . . .*

Scene Five: Break Room

. . . another service. Headphones on, **Alan** *watches it.* **Alannah** *enters.*

Alan   The funeral of P. Richards, fifty-nine. Hospital caretaker from Dundee. The delayed one from a couple weeks back. Not really anything of note other than that his son's about to sing Ave Maria.

Craig *enters. He doesn't realise* **Alannah** *is in the room.*

Craig   Ah! AA. Nice to see Camgirl not chewing the ear off you for once. She set you a price yet?

Alannah   That mean I can invoice you then?

Craig *(realising she's there)*   Shit. I just . . . I came in to watch the Euros. So maybe, you know – boundaried space. We keep it that way.

He puts his headphones on. **Alan** *turns to* **Alannah***.*

Alan   Good date?

Alannah   Yeah, fine, shit, whatever. *(Getting to it.)* So I've been thinking about it and . . . we gonna call this thing or what?

Alan   As in title the investigation? See, I don't even know if 'investigation' is the right word –?

Alannah   As in 'call it'. Think about winding this whole thing down.

Alan   . . . What?

Alannah   Wow. Communicating with you is – *shockingly* – proving difficult. *(Different tack.)* It's just . . . cul de sacs. This whole fucking thing. All it is. If he was findable, he'd be found. I mean, what are we *actually* hoping for here? That some vicar in some church just – what – turns to the camera and gives his home address. Drops a fucking pin. Honestly, the optimal outcome is what?

Alan   No more questions.

Alannah   Oh. It's the total heat death of questions that we're pitching for is it –

Alan   *Your* questions.

Beat.

Alannah   Well, I have my answer, don't I? Have had it for a while now. Someone forced him to do this. And honestly, we should have – . . . we should have clocked out there. Because that's probably what this – . . . this fucker loves, what he *really* loves. People chasing him. *Obsessing* over him. Well, he can fucking . . . just fuck off, you know.

Alan   Don't we have to . . . at least sort of . . . try though, maybe?

Alannah   'At least sort of try though, maybe' . . . Rousing, Alan. Gettysburg awaits. Look, I'm sure it's been *nice* to pretend to Mum you've a non-imaginary pal. But I – . . . This was out of my hands. And now . . . it needs to start getting out of my head. I brought you into this, I now release you. We all move on. Successfully. With an answer. I'll never understand it all but I can . . . find a way to live with that.

Alan   Cos you've got someone else to blame now?

Silence.

Alannah   . . . What the fuck did you just say? (*No response, anger building.*) Wow. I am . . . Fuck, I am really sorry for trying to be nice there because I could have *easily, easily* – . . . Do you know what I think? (*Pointing.*) Your job out there . . . I think you'd do it for free. I mean, we were creating a profile type for Sim, but wow . . . if I'm not eyeballing the cookie cutter 'damaged loner' right now. It . . . *reeks* off you. How much you want *anyone* to tell you that you're important, that you fucking matter. And you know why they never will? Because you, Alan, do-fucking-not.

Alan   Do you know what I think? I think that was a lot of words and none of them answered my question.

He returns to watching the streaming funeral. Puts his headphones back on. Beat.

Alannah   That it? Little man gonna doodle Mummy telling him he's a good boy.

Alan   Don't really do that so much anymore. And no. Just watching this – well *trying* to watch this but the son's Ave Maria keeps glitching.

Alannah   Oh, well, I'm sure you'll find a Samaritans hotline to wank over –

Alan   Gone again.

Craig   Shit.

Alannah's *eye is drawn to* **Craig**.

Alan   Shame. He's actually got quite a good voice.

Alannah *approaches* **Craig**. *She yanks out his headphone jack. All of a sudden the room is filled with an acoustic version of 'Ave Maria'. He's watching the same stream as* **Alan**. *Hearing it,* **Alan** *takes off his headphones. Begins scrolling on his phone.*

Craig   Fuck you at? (*Off her non-response.*) *Bound-ar-ies.* Fuck sake.

He exits.

Alannah   . . . Alan.

Alan (*looking through his phone*)   'Craigdigger'. I think he's – . . . One of Sim One's followers is an anonymous, conspiracy account 'Craigdigger'. I think that's him.

Alannah   *What?* Alan, no. He could *be* Sim fucking One, he could be –

Alan   No, I don't think so. Cos – yeah, only seeing this now – about twenty posts down on Craigdigger's page, there's a photo of the words 'through the looking glass' written in marker on a mirror. But he's accidentally, partially photographed himself.

Said image is displayed.

But he could know something. We can . . . *ask* if he wants to talk.

Beat.

Alannah   Go to the supply closet. Get the cable ties.

Concerned, **Alan** *looks to her.*

Scene Six: Craig's Office

It's a few minutes later. **Craig**, *oblivious, sits in his office on his phone.* **Alan** *enters.*

Craig   Hey mate.

A fire alarm goes.

Oh. Saved by the bell. What's the fire assembly point again?

Alan   The 140 stop. But don't worry, she just set that off to clear the floor.

Craig   Right. (*Processing this, confused.*) . . . What?

Alannah *enters. She locks the door.*

Craig   What's going – sorry, did you just lock that door? *My* door?

Alannah   This is, for now, the *reasonable* approach. (*A cold glance at* **Alan**.) Sim One Says. We know you're 'Craigdigger'. We know you're playing his 'game'. And you're going to tell us everything you know. Right now.

Beat. It all 'lands' for **Craig**.

Craig   Wow. You two. And it's over *this*. Wow. You shake enough trees. But you never can tell which one the spooks are gonna tumble out of. Hope the landing wasn't *too* hard.

Alannah (*looks to* **Alan**)   . . . I *hate* the reasonable approach.

Craig   Look, just tell me who you're with. Straight out. Not gonna be fobbed off with 'sorry, that's classified'. Just won't. (*Off her frustration.*) Oh that's fine. I can stonewall as well as anyone. I'm a fucking – . . . boundary wall in West Clare, love.

Alannah   Fucking *hell*. 'CraigDigger'. Playing the game, just tell us –

Craig   Woah, *sorry*, do not lump me in with those *lemmings*. Okay? I do not 'play'. From the long grass, I assess. See who could be benefitting. See however the fuck he's making them do all this.

Alan   Craig . . . We just want to know if you've corresponded with Sim One. At any point.

Craig   Okay, so if this is *not* bait, if you're *not* just using some rando suicide pool to bring me in on something actually big league, some file on some home hard drive, if you're telling the truth . . . Should be no problem to have a few l'il drinks together. Cos if you're *not* on duty, if you're *not* with someone, shouldn't be an issue with that, should there? (*Off her frustration.*) Look, Dorothy. You wanna find Oz, you wanna get a peek behind the curtain? Then you're gonna need to meet the Tin Man.

He takes out a bunch of cans from his desk. **Alannah** *turns to* **Alan**.

Alannah   This face. That's the signal that we're done with the reasonable fucking approach. (*Off his reticence.*) Alan. We fucking said. *Now.*

She places the cable ties on the desk. Uncomfortable, **Alan** *takes one.*

Alan   Craig, would you either allow me to put this cable tie on you. Or allow us to check your computer –

Alannah   Why are you giving him a drop-down menu, just fucking tie him.

Craig   Oh, you're going to detain me *here*? With surveillance cameras. Empty threat much? (*Places his arm out to be tied.*) Come on, I fucking dare you. I'd *love* to see it. (*Turns to* **Alan**.) Actually, I double dare you. I *treble* –

Alannah *quickly puts a tie on his arm.*

Craig   You fucking bitch! What are you – what the fuck are you doing –

Alan   Alannah, is that maybe a little tight?

Alannah   You noticed.

Craig   No, tell me who you're with. Who you're *really* with, cos I know –

Alan   Craig, her brother was one of the people who died.

Beat. A look of fury from **Alannah**. *That wasn't supposed to be said.* **Craig,** *a bit crestfallen, is realising this isn't what he thought it was.*

Craig   So you're . . . not the apparatus of a deep state?

Alannah   Fucking hell. You are the Dunning–Kruger effect made flesh.

Craig (*correcting, oblivious*)   It's Freddy Krueger. And don't look at me like I'm some kind of simp. There's other hundred per cent pools popping up now. Just like his. But you're the Scooby Doos out there still looking to find this one angry teen in a fucking . . . GameStop of angry teens.

Alan   How do you know it's a teenager?

Beat. **Alan** *pulls* **Craig**'s *phone from his pocket.*

Craig I don't – people have *talked* about meeting him, okay. That's the – . . . ballpark age range. It's . . . consensus, that's all. And I'm not giving my passcode, so you can just go and fucking whistle there, mate –

Alan *holds the phone in front of* **Craig***'s face, it unlocks it.*

Craig Fuck. *Wait* mate, you won't find anything there. So don't make this *even* worse for yourself –

Alan Craig messaged him. A . . . few times. And after the fourth message, they replied, the account replied. But it's been deleted since. (*Looks to him.*) Craig, what did he write to you?

Beat.

Craig Yeah, can't remember.

As **Alannah** *raises a can in threat,* **Alan** *puts out a stilling hand.*

Alan You'd have got his IP address though . . . (*Off his look.*) If he sent you a message on *that* platform, you'd have been able to track it down.

Beat.

Craig You know what . . . think I'm gonna sit tight. Because, what's gonna happen is that – real soon – people are gonna start flocking back up to this floor. And within a minute some dinkus is gonna have some issue with some ticket because some dinkus always does. And they're gonna rap on my door. And I cannot wait to see how that plays out for both of you.

Alan So . . . I don't wish to *threaten* you but –

Craig Oh? Is that because – little Rain Boy – cos maybe you *can't*? Cos you –

Alannah (*seeing the screen*) Oh. *Jesus.* (*Thrown.*) 'Please Sim One, lift me out of all this.' Eh . . . 'Sim One, I can't keep being this much of a nothing, I insist, I beg. 34 Sullivan. C, name me next.' . . . Craig, did you contact him to ask to be –

Craig It's called drawing him out. Okay. Yeah. Playing the long con with it. To see if it's even real . . . so, don't – . . . (*Falling back to it.*) Long. Con.

Alan I was actually talking about the . . . 'For My Eyes Only' folder.

Craig *falls silent.*

Alan . . . Craig . . . the tickets sent to you for assessment. The posts marked for deletion. Have you been . . . *saving* some of them?

Silence.

And then . . . re-posting them? Because the people who are . . . paying us to remove these things. They . . . might not love that.

Beat.

Craig No. *No.* Don't look at me like I'm some – . . . They're not gifs of cats being knifed. It's words. It's . . . things. Being. Said. People being held to account. You wanna live in an airbrushed world with your eyes wide fucking shut. Do it. Be that thing. But I . . . *shan't.* Some of it – . . . matters too much to go. You know, we start burning books. Bodies start to – . . . burning bodies comes pretty shortly afterwards. Someone said that once – a man, a fucking *man* said that once.

Silence.

It's a proxy. The IP address. It's set up so it pings in the wrong place.

Alan Craig. Please tell me the address –

Craig Aberaeron. (*Off his confusion.*) Exactly. A seaside town in Wales. That's where this 'global syndicate' is based. And it's not even Aberaeron. It pings *near* Aberaeron. It's in my last searched, have at it. It's about twenty houses, half a lighthouse and that is fucking *it*. Cos – listen to me – it's a

dummy. Now let me out of this fucking thing. This second.
This *moment* –

Alannah   How far back have you been keeping them . . .?
The tickets.

Beat. She's been processing this all the last while.

Do you have it on there? Laurence's post, the one he put up
before he died. The post Alan deleted. 4 August. 5.23 a.m.

Craig   *What?* Love, two per cent of what's deleted on this
floor goes through quality control and I keep – *maybe* – two
per cent of that –

Alan (*gentle*)   Alannah . . . I know this is important. But
there hasn't been a contestant named this week. We *could* go
there . . . get there by the morning.

Silence.

Craig   Mate. Look at her. She doesn't give a shit.

Alannah *holds the phone up to* **Craig**'*s face again.*

Alannah   Phone lock's off now. Can flick through them all
on the move.

They go to leave.

Craig   Least you can do for me. If your brother's post is
somewhere in there – which it fucking won't be – do let me
know if you and your webcam make an appearance.

He clocks the flicker of vulnerability in her reaction.

. . . What? (*Realising it.*) No. *No.* Now, I mean, I know you're
hardly on the fucking Mensa call-back list but surely you've
put together the potential steps. *Surely.* Even the *possibility.*
He posts a vid. Gets taken down because it contains some
explicit content. And then boom, he checks out. I mean, it
has to have occurred to you. He tops himself. Because he
finally saw you tapping yourself. (*Off her look.*) No. *No.* This
cannot be breaking news.

Alan   Craig, maybe don't –

Craig   Sorry, *sorry*, you of the – Oooh, I'm not *ashamed* of it, doesn't bother me, *sex* positivity, *body* positivity. 'Keep, delete, who gives a shit.' 'Til it *doesn't* suit. That it? 'Well, fuck maybe, maybe I *do* want these things to fall into a sinkhole and never get queefed back out again.'

Beat.

Know what your problem is. You have no idea what you *actually* think about anything. You're just a set of – a patchwork of editorials from the *Huffington Post*. There's no *spark* of originality to you. I mean, Alan here. He's a – no offence – if this is the Life Awards, the *Existence* awards, that's a seat filler right there. But he knows what he is. Me, I'm a watcher on the wall. I'll say it proud. Whereas you, *you* –

She picks up a can.

Oh go on. Please, *please* go right ahead and prove my point that you've not a single iota to say back to any of that. Go on then.

He juts out his chin, inviting her to throw it at him. She empties it over him.

(*Still unfazed.*) Oooh. Did you see that? She's flipped convention on its head. Convention's *dizzy* around her. Brave. Brilliant. *Bold.*

Alannah *goes.* **Craig** *turns to* **Alan**.

Craig   She'll chew you out, mate. Trust me. You'll think she has your hand. Only good at playing with herself, she is.

Alan *goes. In the silence, a still tied* **Craig** *sits. He reaches down. Grabs one of the cans from the floor. He opens it.*

Scene Seven: Boat

A ferry to Holyhead. **Alan** *is on deck.* **Alannah** *arrives in with two high-vis vests.*

Alannah   Found them below deck. The IP address narrows it down to like . . . a few streets right? (*Off* **Alan***'s nod.*) Sim's message to Craig came from a TalkTalk server, so we say we're from TalkTalk. That way, we *know* off the bat if that house could be the sender. Then we upsell them on something, invite ourselves in.

Alan   Upsell them on . . . which exactly?

Alannah   *Bundles,* I don't know. We'll figure it out as we go.

Alan   Could we . . . figure it out *before* we go?

Alannah (*sharp*)   Fine, you lead the fucking way for once.

Beat.

What?

Alan   Does this not all feel a bit . . . odd? I mean . . . if Sim One is here. Why would he make himself so . . . easy for someone to find?

Alannah   Jesus. Easy to fucking find? Is there a gift horse alive that you *won't* look in the fucking teeth?

Beat.

Alan   Is Laurence's post on the –

Alannah (*shutting it down*)   Still checking, okay.

Silence. A message from **Tina** *comes in.*

Tina (*speaking her messages*)   Heading out now.

Alan (*speaking his messages*)   Okay. Out where?

Tina   Meeting Graham. Just getting a taxi.

Alan   Mum, I'm so sorry. I forgot that was tonight.

Beat.

Alan   Good luck.

Beat.

Are you nervous?

Tina   No.

Beat.

Yes.

Have a good night, love.

Tina *goes.* **Alan** *makes a grimace.* **Alannah** *clocks it.*

Alannah   . . . What?

Alan *shows her the message exchange.*

Alannah   Jesus. When was the last time she went on one of these?

Alan   Eh . . . I don't know if she and my dad ever went out on dates.

Silence. With the tension still in the air, **Alannah** *takes the moment for a reset.*

Alannah   This is probably the part where we address earlier. In the break room. Wipe the slate clean. Happy to give that a miss if you are.

Alan   Okay. (*Tentative.*) Would it be alright if I still said sorry anyway –

Alannah   Why? Not like you said anything about us that wasn't – . . . (*A sigh.*) Me and Laurence, we used to send each other . . . we call them 'dick pics'. Photos of Dick Van Dyke. And three months before he died, I sent him a photo of Mr Van Dyke papped outside an Applebee's. Which was my last message to him. I . . . think I mistake correspondence for contact sometimes. But in the end . . . it's all past tense now. Making this all more than a little pointless.

Alan   Can I say a – . . .? (*Off her expression.*) Okay, I can, noted. If you really think it's pointless, I'm just . . . a bit surprised you're still here.

Alannah   Well, I dunno. Maybe Sim being found will explain it all. Maybe stopping him – even once – it pulls down a whole network, makes every suicide pool dry up. I mean, it won't, but . . .

Beat.

The truth is . . . I feel like a non-person a lot of the time. Actually, no. A pre-person. And it's never been as loud as when I'm standing next to you. And I could say I'm still here cos it's to honour Laurence. But I . . . I think I just want to see if I can feel a bit less shit really.

Beat.

A bit less 'Alannah Allsorts'.

Off his look.

. . . Nickname.

Beat.

Ferries are weird.

Lights.

Scene Eight: Aberaeron

Alan *and* **Alannah** *are at a doorway. The end of a 'sales pitch'.*

Alan   Well, we at TalkTalk thank you for your time today –

The door is closed on them. As they move to the next house:

Alannah   God, need a piss in a very real way.

Alan   Didn't you just go at that cafe –

Alannah   I piss a lot.

She knocks on a door. **Lauren** *answers. She's wiping her face with a towel.*

Lauren   Hi. Excuse the musk, just finished a shift.

Alan   Hi. We're from TalkTalk and we have an . . . *exciting* new –

Lauren   Sorry. My husband actually works for Vodafone. So we already – . . . you'd sort of be selling ice to Eskimos.

Beat.

Alan   Could she maybe do a wee here?

Lauren   Eh . . . well, the place is a bit of a . . . I should really say the tip is a bit of a place at the moment. But . . . sure. Third door on the left upstairs. You can use the odour from Jason's room as a homing beacon.

Alannah   . . . Thanks.

Lauren *goes into the house.* **Alannah** *does too. The scene, with no gap in time, shifts to . . .*

Scene Nine: Lauren's House

. . . inside the house. Awkward, **Alan** *stands outside.* **Lauren** *looks on.*

Lauren   Can get out of the sun, if you'd like. I used to door-to-door for Oxfam. So feel your pain. Of course, that'll mean standing nearer to Sweaty Betty though so . . . pick your pain.

Alan (*entering*)   Thank you, Betty.

Lauren   Oh, I'm Lauren. Sweaty Betty was a – . . . (*He's embarrassed.*) It's okay.

Beat. **Alannah** *arrives back downstairs.*

Alannah   Thank you *so* much for that.

Alan   We can probably let Miss . . .

Lauren   Donnellan. But, again, Lauren is fine.

Alan   We should probably let Lauren have the rest of her afternoon –

Alannah   See, I was wondering if we might be able to take up a fraction more of it. Sorry. The old . . . bathroom ruse. Gets our foot in the door. (*Off* **Alan**'s *look*.) He hates it. Still a bit green, you see.

Lauren   Oh.

Alannah   So . . . Yes. You're covered for TV and broadband *but* . . . how would you feel about twice the connection speed. And reliability. For free. We – TalkTalk – are trialling something in the area. *And*, if you sit down with us, a free . . . *mug*.

Lauren   (*a lengthy sigh*)   Go on then. I'd murder a cup of tea. And this gives me an excuse to 'resort' to ordering takeout.

Alannah   Big old horde to feed?

Lauren   Six-year-old twins. A coeliac husband. And a thirteen-year-old on 'a bulk'.

She goes to the kitchen.

Alannah   If he's like the thirteen-year-olds I know, I assume he'd be the main consumer of your internet is he?

Alannah *sends* **Alan** *a message. A photo of a thirteen-year-old boy's bedroom. On his desk, there's a laptop. A TalkTalk dongle.*

Lauren   (*offstage*)   Jason's certainly the main *complainer* about it.

Alannah   (*responding to* **Lauren**, *feigning conviviality*)   Ha. Naturally. (*Hushed, to* **Alan**.) TalkTalk dongle in his room. Teenager, just about. So let's just see if his laptop has anything – . . . (*Clocking* **Alan**'s *expression*.) What?

Alan   . . . Orbs.

He takes the phone, zooms in another part of the bedroom photo. A black and white poster of Nina Simone. He zooms in further. To the top left of the picture. Four stage lights against a black background. It's the SimOne.Says avatar orbs. The exact same ones.

Alannah (*audible*)   Fuck.

Lauren (*offstage*)   All good?

Alannah (*calling back*)   Yeah, sorry.

Alannah *and* **Alan** *look at each other. This is the place. Beat.*

Alannah (*calling back to* **Lauren**)   Right. So four o'clock, Jason would probably be homeward bound soon enough then, would he?

Lauren *emerges with a tray of tea and digestive biscuits.*

Lauren   Yes but much to his disappointment, he probably *won't* be the major decision maker for the broadband though.

Alannah   Ha. Of course. Oh wow, this is top-tier treatment here.

Lauren   Only took 'em out of a packet, didn't stay up all night stencilling them. (*Polite.*) So . . . getting better, free wi-fi? You've a tired but captive audience.

Alannah   Yes. Yes. *First* thing I'd like to do . . . is compare your present connection speed with our upgrade. Would there maybe be a . . . device in the house that I could use to eh – . . . to show that.

Alan   Not a phone.

Lauren   Sure.

She pulls a laptop from her bag.

Alannah   Great. That is great. (*Sees it.*) Bet you're super-grateful to whichever of your kids stuck the LSD sticker and the Tame Impala magnet on that. (*Casual.*) But you know what. What I'm realising. Forgot the testing dongle. Yeah, left it in the car. Plus, *plus* you're owed a mug, I believe. So –

(*Patting pockets.*) *Keys* . . . Crap. I think . . . *Ugh.* I bet I bloody well set them down in the bathroom and – . . . Sorry, can hopefully screw my head on too when I'm up there. Alan, why don't you talk her through the . . . science of the fibreoptic trial scheme. Good experience for you.

She starts to head towards the stairs.

Lauren   I'm assuming that you're the bereaved, yes?

Beat.

I'm right in saying that? (*Off her look.*) So, I think you're about to go into my son's room. And take something, his laptop probably, cos he took a dongle he's not supposed to be using. And that's not really something I'm willing to let you do. Now, you don't need to sit back down. But maybe you'd step back towards here please.

Beat. **Alannah** *doesn't move.*

Lauren   So, I'm going to show your colleague something.

She opens her laptop. Clicks into a specific tab, shows it to **Alan**.

Alan   It's the . . . log-in page for the Sim One account.

Lauren   On *my* laptop. So we can all agree, no need to go upstairs.

Beat. **Alannah** *takes a step back from the stairs.*

Lauren   Now, whenever you feel ready, could you tell me the name of the person you've lost please? (*Off her non-response.*) This isn't a trap. I just want to be as specific with you as possible. And to do that, I need you to be specific with me.

Alan   We never saw his name going up –

Alannah   Alan, shut the fuck up.

Lauren   Right. But he followed the account, and you think his name *was* posted at some point, yes? (*Off her silence.*) I'm not aiming to laugh at you or show you something horrible. I think this – all this – it's revolting.

Beat.

Alannah   Laurence Baker.

Lauren   Baker L. Do you have the date? And age.

Alannah   4 August. Thirty-three.

Lauren   Thirty-three Baker L. Now . . . I don't think I ever posted that name. But I'm gonna open a list on this. (*Gestures to the laptop.*) And your friend – . . .

Alan   Alan.

Lauren   . . . they're your actual names? (*He nods.*) Okay. (*Checks laptop.*) Yeah. So haven't touched this. Only opened it. And Alan here can tell you if your brother was –

Alannah   Stop talking.

Alan *scrolls through it. And then . . . he turns to* **Alannah.** *Shakes his head. A beat.*

Lauren   That happens, I'm afraid. People who sign up, who follow it, they – . . . well, they don't always wait for Simone to say so. I'm not trying to be glib. It's just how it happens.

Alan (*pointing to the sticker on her laptop*)   LSD is . . . Lauren –

Lauren   Lauren Simone Donnellan, yes. (*To* **Alannah.**) Would you maybe like to sit now?

Alannah *doesn't move. Just holds her stare. Silence.*

Lauren   So, I'm a paramedic. Sometimes in my work, people, they can get angry with us for finding bodies too late. And that's not in cases when it's minutes in the difference, it's when they've been sat there for days. Undiscovered. I suspect that's a bit of guilt peeking out. That *they* didn't –

Alannah   Can you get to a point.

Lauren   What I'm trying to say is that it's even harder on you if you were an absent sister.

Alannah *grabs the butter knife on the table.* **Lauren** *remains calm.*

Lauren   So . . . I think you'd be a while at me with that, love. Okay.

Silence. **Alannah** *loosens her grip on the knife. Limply, she places it down.*

(*To* **Alan**.) You're just a friend? (*He nods.*) . . . Alan?

Alan   Kenedy. One 'n'.

Lauren   And, Alan Kenedy, what is it you do?

Alan   I – *we* work in content moderation. (*As she goes to talk.*) Are you actually making people do this?

Lauren   Oh. No. No, I can't 'make' – . . . .I'm not capable of it. That's not said in a self-protecting way, it's the truth. They all have the reasons for 'why' already. When I do a naming this week, what they'll be getting from me – the sum total – is the 'when'. That's it. (*Getting to it.*) It's okay. I'm going to talk you through all this. But – and this is important to say – nothing that you say can convince me that this isn't exactly what we need to do. For my kids, you, all of us. But it's likely going to be hard for you to hear. Because . . . it's awful. It is. (*To* **Alannah**.) So you can leave if you like. No judgement. I can talk to Alan. And he can say it all in time.

Alannah *doesn't move.* **Lauren** *sees she's made her decision.*

Lauren   Few years ago, there was a story about a Malaysian girl. She was sixteen. Likely not well. And this poor girl, she put up a poll online. Asked one question. 'D or L'. It went viral – . . . you remember this, don't you? You probably had to remove content related to the – . . . (**Alan** *nods.*) So you know it didn't go viral because people flocked to her aid and chose 'life' for her. Clicked the 'L' button.

And it was a story for a . . . *day* maybe. Her death. Because things like it . . . they regularly happen. She is *not* an outlier. The bombardment of technology, other people's chatter into our daily lives, it's . . . altering the development of people's brain stems. Kids are having episodes akin to a mid-life crisis at the age of fifteen. Been chronicled in multiple medical journals. Neuroscientific fact. But . . . we're not sleepwalking into this. Because, at the same time, this world is running out. *We're* running it out. And unfulfilment – it's funny – unfulfilment, loneliness, unhappiness. It created the socials. But thing is . . . that unhappiness is also how we're going to get ourselves out of it too. Cos it's what's drawn them to all this.

We are ticking *past* midnight. It's too far gone. And there is no one coming over the hill on horseback to save us. So what we'll need is for the resources we have left to stretch further. And so we need to accept our obvious *solution*. Which is to have less of us. And there is – unfortunately – a ready-made group there. A first cab off the rank. And it's not the poor fuckers that I see fighting for their lives in the back of my ambulance or the ones clinging to life in neonatal wards. It's the ones existing in an overwhelming world that they now want to stop spinning.

She dabs her eye with a tissue.

Sorry . . . (*Half to herself.*) The shit you have to say. (*A composing breath.*) You know, I always said if one of my lot began to follow the account – happened across it – I wouldn't treat them any differently to the others. But I know I wouldn't be able to follow through on that. Absolute hypocrite on top of everything else.

Alannah   This is fucking mental –

Lauren   You haven't really let me finish yet though, have you?

Alan   It can't just be putting up names. Before this, there
were hundreds of pools like these and they didn't all – . . .

Lauren   The rate of follow-through? (**Alan** *nods*.) I won't
congratulate myself because at the end of the day, it is what it
is, it's something appalling. But yes, the method is effective.
Particularly.

Beat.

I'd a call-out once. It was a welfare check. After some
prolonged inactivity from a farmhouse. We get there. It's all
the usual tell-tale signs, stepping over days of front porch
post. And we – myself and my shift partner Jess – we find the
farmer in his shed. Bring him down. And take him to Prince
Philip General Hospital. Jess drives. Because I'm – well, I'm
in floods. Always am at these things.

Anyway, the farmer. Turns out his daughter, she works in the
cafeteria of the Prince Philip. And after we bring her dad to
the morgue, she's the one serving us our cokes. And until
someone contacts her that evening, she's no idea what we
know. And that . . . sits with me. How I see death daily. But
that I'm also very often the *first* to see it. And – when I'm
back in the ambulance – it starts to go around my head. The
idea. (*A sigh*.) Forgive me for this format, but it seems to be
the . . . easiest. To follow anyway.

Beat. Another sigh. This isn't easy. And then . . . she goes into it.

So Step 1: *Set up but stand out*. Easy part, you create an
account. Well, *accounts*. You only know one, the most
popular one. But you need fallbacks, in case. Same time, you
start whispers in the right forums. But make them work to
find you. People like the feeling of exclusivity.

Step 2: *Use access to show success*. So I picked a call-out. And
right after I'd left the house of the lady who'd died, I posted
their name. But . . . if you can gain access to hospital
databases you can put up names from all over the world.
Before it's public that they're dead. Prior to the first name,

the account has a few sets of eyeballs. After I post the first funeral. They multiply.

Step 3: *Repeat and delete.* You do that method – that kind of cheat method – about . . . five to eight times. But every time, you delete the post. See when you delete – sorry to inform you of this with your line of work – it just makes people grab for it more. And for every repeat . . . those pairs of eyeballs are growing exponentially. Cos it's getting out now. About this lone pool with the hundred per cent follow-through rate. And then . . . when you've hit a certain point, when you believe you've a high enough level of buy-in . . .

Step 4 . . .

Alan   . . . you test it.

Lauren (*approving*)   *Time to test it.* You pick a name. An early adopter. Someone who believes in this thing that has a hundred per cent follow-through rate. Someone unhappy who wants you to take the wheel. You name them as a contestant. And when you see how unquestioningly they – . . . (*Struggling.*) Christ. Sorry. (*Composing herself.*) And it's just about picking well from that point onwards. And then . . . there is a final step. Because, well, yeah, I'm only one person.

Step 5: *Expand.* Pick out a few people, ones you've been monitoring. You maybe make contact. Or let them find you. A lot of the time, it's been people who actively seek it out. Death. In their day to day. And, well . . . you sit them down. You talk them through steps 1 through 4. You invite them to start their own account. To put their own . . . *inflection* on it. If that gets up and running, they do the same with others. Then those others . . . well, you can fill it in from there. And it won't be solved with our generation. It won't. It can't. But we can show them a 'path'. So we can overcome all this. Eventually.

Beat.

Sorry for laying it out like that. But it's what sticks. Apparently.

Silence. **Alannah** *gets to her feet. At the door, she stops and turns to* **Lauren**.

Alannah   Die fucking roaring.

She goes. A silence and then . . .

Alan   . . . With the names . . . do you have an amount that's enough?

Beat.

Lauren (*checking watch*)   They're almost home. Sorry.

Beat. As **Alan** *goes to leave,* **Lauren** *types something into her laptop.*

You know, some people . . . they want to help. It just leaps out from them. Never let anyone tell you that it's not a brilliant thing to have. And I have a feeling, nothing more . . . that you could do this, Alan.

You *could* do this. But pulling this string. It's not for everyone. I mean, your friend could. But another instinct tells me that you might be built to help in other ways. And you *can* help. And I suspect you've always wanted to. Maybe even felt a bit . . . 'fated' to do it. But you've maybe just never known what that is.

She hits send. **Alan**'s *phone buzzes. It flashes up. A new post from SimOne.Says: 'Tonight's Contestant is 23 Kenedy A.'*

Alan *looks at his phone. Silence. He looks at her. Their eyes meet.*

Lauren   . . . I'm so sorry.

Beat. A slightly stunned **Alan** *walks out.*

Scene Ten: Outside Lauren's

Alannah *sits on a wall.* **Alan** *approaches. Silence.*

Alannah   Fucking psycho . . . Don't give a shit he wasn't on her fucking list, she can fucking – . . .

Beat.

It's not on Craig's phone. Whatever Laurence posted before he died. Checked three times. So . . . that's that then.

Beat.

I don't *think* it was something of me, don't think that was his style. Plus, you'd remember deleting it. Something like that, even you.

Beat.

I did the stupidest fucking thing a while ago. I started to . . . think about what I'd like it to have been. The video. As though I could . . . choose. I wanted it to be something from when we were kids. Us together. Choir or . . . I don't know. But whatever it was, doesn't really matter. I know what he thought about me. Cos he didn't call that day. And the likelihood is, what the smart money says is that he didn't cos he knew I'd find a way not to be there.

Beat.

And he *was* smart. About me.

Beat.

I don't expect – . . . I know they don't go away. The questions. But do you ever let yourself ask . . . easier ones?

Alan   Eh . . .

Alannah   . . . What?

Alan   Not really, no.

She looks at him. A seeming invitation to talk. He weighs it up. Decides to say it.

Eh . . . my dad . . . he died when I was younger. He wasn't the easiest. On us. And probably himself. But he . . . the night he did it, he told us that, eh . . . 'None of us add value.' The three of us. So that question . . . still . . . yeah.

Silence.

Alannah   Should make a . . . report on her. You're good to do that, yeah?

Silence.

Alan   Sure.

Alannah   Hope they . . . you know, do something about her. This time.

Beat.

You've got a shift, don't you? Today. I'll – . . . Don't think I'll go in for mine. Might get the later ferry back.

Beat.

Might head on actually. If that's okay. And, eh . . . yeah. Sorry about all that, with your – . . . Sounds hard.

Alan   . . . Drank plenty of water.

Alannah   What? (*Remembering the call-back.*) Oh, yeah. Right.

Beat.

Yeah.

Beat.

I'll get you back for the ferry. I'll send that on.

Beat.

Cheers.

She goes. Beat. **Alan** *re-reads the post from SimOne.Says:* 'Tonight's Contestant is 23 Kenedy A.'

Scene Eleven: Work

Alan *finds himself back at his workstation. He turns on his screen. The usual 'Thank You for Making the Internet Safer' screed hits him. And then, a malign, black and white pixelated image comes up. He stares at it. The will to do anything, it's not there anymore. Instead, he just stares at it in all its horror.*

Craig *enters.*

Craig   Heeeeey, matey. Do you've a minute?

Beat.

Wanted to, you know, check in. Have we heard from herself at all today? Alannah.

Beat.

They found me like that, you know. That way. Yesterday. (*Off his non-response.*) Kept you out of it though, so . . . You're good. All is . . . 'in balance' again.

Beat.

I'll be honest, mate . . . I really need this job. All that . . . extracurricular stuff. That's in the bin now. Plugged out from all that. It's actually childish, you know. Cos . . . this is why . . . Your five years here, my . . . time here. That's why we add – . . . That's our purpose, you know. This. *This.* The 'binmen'.

Beat.

Could chat to them about getting you into a supervisor role. Could do that. Be nice to actually have a . . . Think we'd be good. As a duo, you know.

Beat.

Does anyone here like me? I mean . . . if I wasn't – . . .

Beat.

Sorry . . . stupid question.

Beat. Then a look from **Craig***: '. . . Right?' Silence.* **Alan** *leaves.*

Scene Twelve: Home

Alan *enters. No one else seems to be home.*

Alan (*seeing if she's home*)   . . . Mum?

No response. Beat. He begins a message.

Alan (*speaking the message*)   Hi, Mum, are you home soon, cos I –

He starts again. Tries to sound less lost.

Alan (*speaking the message*)   Hi, Mum, sorry to bother you but I think I might need some –

He stops. Reconsiders. And then.

Alan (*speaking the message*)   Hope it went great, Mum.

Beat. He takes out his phone and re-reads the SimOne.Says post: 'Tonight's Contestant is 23 Kenedy A.'

And then . . . it gets deleted. He stares at it. It seems to be a sign.

The 'bad' content colours start to cloud the room. A moment of uncertainty. And then . . . he puts his phone on a tripod. It should feel ambiguous if this is an 'instructional' or if he's emulating the opening with Laurence. He hits record.

He stands there. In total uncertainty.

Alan   . . . Don't know what step this is.

His phone rings. He answers.

Alan   Hi, Mum . . . (*Hearing it's not his mum.*) Oh, hi, Graham. (*Hearing that he has her phone.*) Yeah, it's okay I'll . . . I'll tell her that you have her phone. Thanks. (*Hearing that it's good that he's calm.*) Eh . . . yeah, thanks. Sorry, why wouldn't I be calm? (*A longer answer. Detailing what happened this morning.*) . . . Which hospital?

Lights.

Scene Thirteen: Hospital

Alan *enters.* **Tina** *is in a hospital bed.*

Alan   My phone died on the way in, I'm sorry I –

Tina   It's okay, it's okay. Just fainted and got a head bump. It was probably just a . . . build-up. Fatigue. Probably looked worse than it was.

Alan   Did he bring you in?

Tina   He offered to come with me in the ambulance. This morning. It was good of him.

Beat.

Love, I think the visiting hours are . . . they're finishing now.

Alan   Right.

Tina   But you go on. I'll be discharged in a few hours.

Alan   You're . . . doing alright though, yeah?

Tina   Yeah.

Beat. **Alan** *goes to get up. Goes to leave. But as he does, she can't keep it in.*

Tina   Well, actually no, I don't have a clue what shit they're gonna come through those doors and tell me. I never fucking do.

Beat. She has immediate remorse for the 'overshare'.

It's okay, love, you can . . . I'm sorry about that, you can go. I'm – . . . I'm really fine.

Beat.

Alan   Do you always feel like that, Mum?

Tina   Eh . . . I try not to Alan, I really fucking do. (*Decides to keep talking.*) I thought it'd go away. A bit. Now that you . . . need me a little less – a *lot* less. But it's . . . I'm actually a bit more alone with it now.

Beat.

It's okay, love. You don't need to be –

Alan   Mum for the last five years, I've done a job where I watch videos of people dying. A lot of the time, doing it to themselves. Other stuff too. And then I delete them.

It just comes out. Silence. Some processing. More silence. And then.

Tina   Did you say five years? (*A nod.*) Okay.

Alan   I shouldn't be – . . . you're here and . . . I shouldn't be telling you this now.

Tina   It's okay. I don't – . . . I don't know why you haven't told me before.

Alan   Because I shouldn't still – . . . need you like this.

Tina   I still have a Garfield Pez dispenser my dad got me when I was seven. I still squeeze it sometimes.

Beat.

So you do this job. You delete things. So other people don't have to see them? (*A nod.*) But *you* do, Alan.

Alan   I'm good at it.

Tina   Why are you good at it?

Silence.

Alan   Just am.

Silence.

Mum . . . do I add value?

He sees the pain in her reaction to the question. Silence.

Sorry.

Tina   . . . It's alright.

Silence.

You know, I didn't think I could ever miss that time. With him. But all this, it was somehow so much easier when you were ten. And we could just doodle under the table together.

Just . . . shut it all out. Or I could just pick you up. And run you out of the house to . . . wherever we needed to go, wherever felt safe. I could just do that with you.

Beat.

Do you add value . . . So he said it to me too. To both of us. So let me ask you this. Do *I* add value, Alan?

Alan   Of course.

Tina   Too fucking right, I do. And *you* . . .

Silence.

I used to dream about you, you know. When I was pregnant. What you'd be like. Have dreams where I'd talk to you. And then you came along. And you are, darling, beyond the best of my imagination.

She pulls out a hospital chart. Flips it over to a blank sheet.

Alright. So you might not want to talk yet. But something's obviously afoot. And we've already established I can't carry you anymore. You're fucking massive. So . . . you start us off.

She holds out a pen to him.

Come on. He's dropping in my phone soon.

Alan   Mum, I shouldn't have to still –

Tina   Garfield. Pez. Dispenser.

Beat. **Alan** *begins to draw. It's the outline of a kangaroo.*

Tina   Is that a roo? Only thing I could ever bloody draw. (*Watching his progress.*) Wow . . . you still sort of make shit of the ears, don't you?

A small laugh from him. Beat. He hands her the pen. **Tina** *draws a joey in the pouch of the kangaroo. A look between them.*

In the moments after, **Jean** *reappears.* **Alan** *is presented with his notebook again. Appreciative, he takes it from* **Jean.**

Scene Fourteen: Home

Alan *comes home. He takes down the tripod stand. And begins charging his phone. As he does . . . a multitude of pings. A litany of missed calls and messages come through. All from* **Alannah**. *The most recent one is a video message.*

Alannah (*het up*)   Right, right, I've called, messaged and I – . . . nothing. So I don't know why the fuck I'm doing this. I saw – for a split-second I saw she'd posted what I *think* was your name, but then it was fucking gone and I . . . don't know if it definitely *was* you. And I – . . . I'm waiting for a fucking Costa Coffee interview. And I – . . . Fuck this. I'm going to your house. Now. Moving now.

She starts moving.

If it *was* your name, if it *was* you, you are going to fucking listen to this. Cos I – (*Clearing throat.*) Step One: Break her chain. Right now, in this moment, you have the power to – God, I am shit at this.

The air goes out of her pretty quickly.

Don't die. That's the . . . extent of them. My steps.

Beat.

I don't know how to do this bit. Where you actually stick around. I mean, we can even do that podcast if you like. Alert everyone about her. I mean, I wouldn't listen. But we can. It's just, the thing about – . . . (*Can't find more coded language.*) I'll just fucking say it – 'trying to be friends' . . . Is that I'm guessing it works best under a specific condition. Namely, that we're both still here.

Beat.

I'm coming to your house. And there's an outside, remote chance that I'll do better next time. So please just . . . yeah. Be there. Or . . . be anywhere. Please. If you wouldn't mind.

From one AA to another.

The message ends. **Alan** *sits there a moment. An alert comes up on the screen: 'Phone Storage at Capacity – Do You Wish to Delete Video?'*

Alan *looks at it. He deliberates. A small smile. A knock on the door. He looks at it.* **Jean** *indicates he should answer it. A deep breath from* **Alan**. *And . . .*

Lights.

Made in United States
Orlando, FL
22 March 2026

79568394R00056